THE KINGFISHER
CHILDREN'S ENCYCLOPEDIA

GENERAL EDITOR: JOHN PATON

VOLUME 6
LEBANON *to* NERVE

Kingfisher Books, Grisewood & Dempsey Ltd,
Elsley House, 24–30 Great Titchfield Street,
London W1P 7AD

First published in 1989 by Kingfisher Books
Reprinted 1989, 1991, 1992 (with revisions)

BRITISH LIBRARY CATALOGUING
IN PUBLICATION DATA

Kingfisher children's encyclopedia.
1. Children's encyclopedias in English
I. Paton, John, 1914–
032

ISBN 0 86272 467 8

Typesetting: Tradespools Ltd., Frome,
Somerset
Printed in Hong Kong

THE SUBJECT SYMBOLS

Each entry in this encyclopedia has its own easily-recognized symbol opposite the heading. This symbol tells you at a glance which area of interest the entry falls into – is it animals, history or science? Below are the 16 subject areas we have used. At the back of the work there is a list of all the articles divided into subject areas.

PLANTS AND FOOD From microscopic plants to gigantic trees – what they are, how they grow, the food they provide.

THE ARTS Drawing, painting, sculpture, crafts, ballet, modern dance, drama, theatre, TV, cinema etc., plus the great artists.

PEOPLES AND GOVERNMENT Descriptions of peoples of the world, the things they do and the way they govern their countries.

LANGUAGE AND LITERATURE How language is constructed plus descriptions of great playwrights, novelists, poets etc.

SPORTS AND PASTIMES Competitive sports, great athletes and sporting stars plus descriptions of many hobbies.

ASTRONOMY AND SPACE Birth of the Universe, the solar system, galaxies, space exploration etc.

SCIENCE How science is applied in everyday life, the elements, sources of energy, important scientists etc.

RELIGION, PHILOSOPHY AND MYTH How these have changed through history and the ones that have survived.

ANIMALS Descriptions of behaviour, homes and individual species: mammals, birds, reptiles, fishes, insects etc.

MACHINES AND MECHANISMS Explanations of everything from simple machines to jet engines plus descriptions of their inventors.

TRAVEL AND TRANSPORT The history and development of aircraft, ships, railways, cars, motorcycles etc.

HUMAN BODY How the body works, the process of birth, ageing, diseases, immunity, genetics etc.

BUILDINGS The history and development of architecture, modern construction and design, famous buildings and architects etc.

OUR EARTH How the Earth was formed, and how it is still changing, its deserts, mountains, oceans, rivers etc.

HISTORY Great events and great figures from ancient civilizations up to the present day.

COUNTRIES AND PLACES Descriptions, flags, maps, essential statistics etc. for all countries plus places of interest.

Lebanon

Lebanon is a Middle Eastern country bordering on the Mediterranean Sea. It is sandwiched between Syria and Israel. Lebanon's coast is flat, but most of the country inland is mountainous.

Lebanon has been a trading centre for centuries. Ancient Lebanon was part of the Phoenician empire. The Phoenicians were great traders all over the Mediterranean. Later, Lebanon became part of the Byzantine empire, ruled from Constantinople. It was famous for the fine cedar wood that came from its forests.

In recent years the country has become a battleground for a number of religious and political opponents.

LEBANON

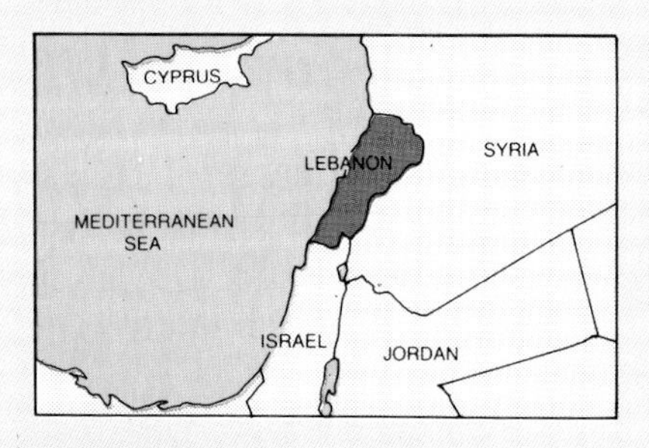

Government: Parliamentary republic
Capital: Beirut
Area: 10,400 sq km
Population: 2,701,000
Language: Arabic
Currency: Lebanese pound

◀ *Lebanon has a rich and exciting history. This fortress at Sidon was built during the Crusades.*

Legend

Legends are stories that are told as true, but cannot be proved. They may have some truth in them, and may be about a real person or place. But they are usually made-up stories. The adventures of Robin Hood and King Arthur are legends.

Lenin, Vladimir

Vladimir Ilyich Lenin (1870–1924) helped to make Russia the first communist country in the world. Before his time, Russia was ruled by emperors, or

▲ *Lenin's revolutionary ideas united the group of communists called Bolsheviks, who overthrew the Russian government in 1917.*

SHORT SIGHTEDNESS

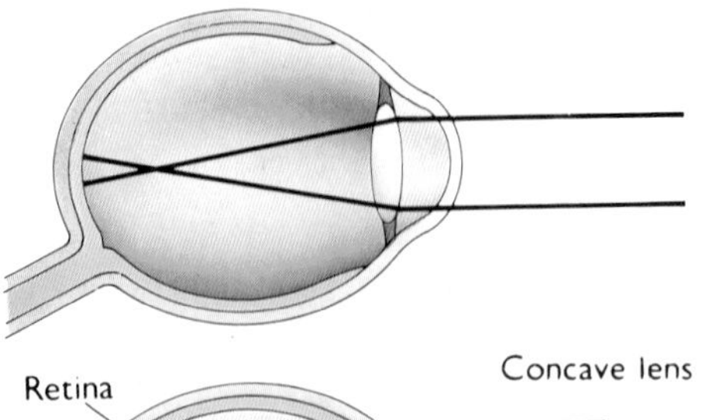

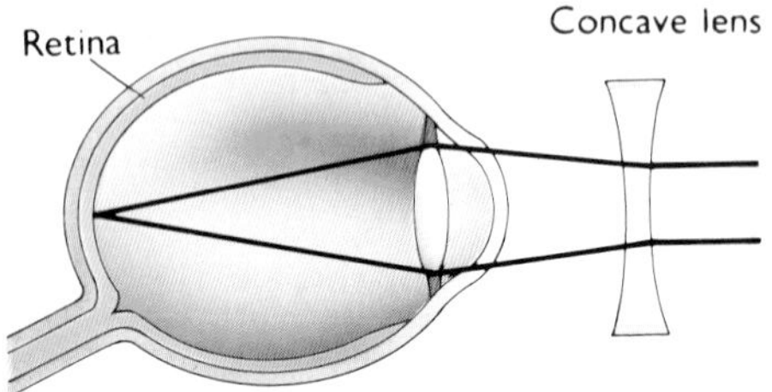

LONG SIGHTEDNESS

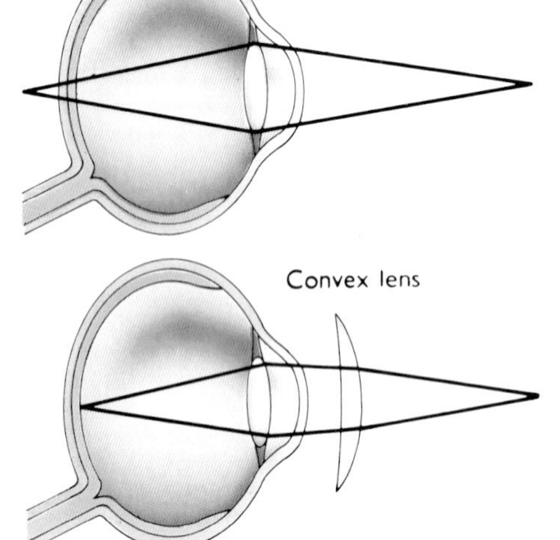

▲ *In people with short sight, light from a distant object is focused by the lens of the eye before it reaches the back of the eye, or retina. This means the object looks blurred. In people with long sight, light from nearby objects is focused at a point beyond the retina, so they appear blurred. Corrective lenses in glasses make the images focus on the retina, so they look sharp and clear.*

tsars. Like Karl MARX, Lenin believed in COMMUNISM. He wanted every country run by the workers and no longer split into rich and poor groups. For many years Lenin lived outside Russia. He wrote books, and articles for communist newspapers. In 1917 he went back to Russia. He became the leader of a group of communists called Bolsheviks, who overthrew the government. Lenin then ruled Russia until he died.

Lens

Lenses are used to make things look bigger or smaller. They are usually made of glass or plastic. The lens inside your EYE is made of PROTEIN. Sometimes eye lenses do not work properly. Then people cannot see clearly. The lenses in spectacles make people's eyesight better. The lenses in MICROSCOPES, binoculars and TELESCOPES make faraway things or small things seem much larger.

Each lens has two smooth sides. Both sides may be curved, or one may be curved and the other flat. There are two main kinds of lens. Lenses where the edges are thicker than the middle are called *concave* lenses. Concave means 'hollowed out'. When LIGHT rays pass through a concave lens, they spread out. If you look at something through a concave lens, it looks smaller than it really is.

Lenses where the middle is thicker than the edges

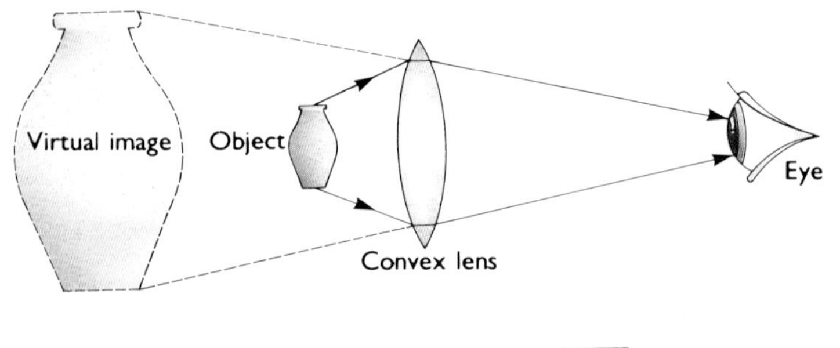

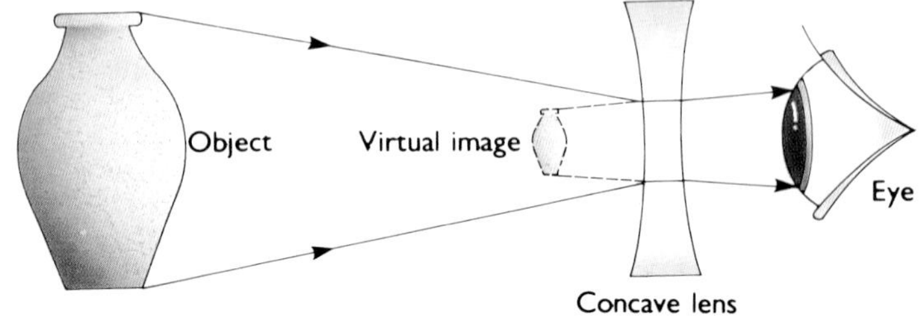

► *Light rays passing through a convex lens bend outwards, making the virtual image appear larger than it really is. The virtual image is what we see. A concave lens bends the rays inwards and the image looks smaller.*

are called *convex* lenses. Convex means 'rounded'. When light rays pass through a convex lens, they come together. If you look at things through a convex lens, they seem larger.

Craftspeople who make lenses know exactly how to shape them for various uses. They may fit different lenses together or shape each side of a lens differently. Short-sighted people use spectacles that have concave lenses. People with long sight have spectacles with convex lenses.

The 'burning glass' for producing fire from the Sun's rays has been known since ancient times. The magnifying property of a simple lens was recorded by Roger Bacon in the 13th century. Spectacle lenses were first used in the 14th century, and by the 16th century spectacles were commonly used. Benjamin Franklin invented the bifocal lens in 1760.

Leonardo da Vinci

Leonardo da Vinci (1452–1519) was an Italian artist and inventor. He lived during the RENAISSANCE. One of his most famous paintings is the *Mona Lisa*. It is a picture of a woman who is smiling mysteriously. Many people have wondered what she was smiling at. Leonardo made thousands of drawings of

◀ *Leonardo's famous painting, the* Mona Lisa, *hangs in the Louvre museum in Paris.*

▼ *Leonardo's self-portrait, drawn in about 1512, is the only known authentic likeness of the artist.*

Leonardo often smoothed in the paint with his fingers to get a special effect. The result is that several of the great artist's paintings have clearly visible fingerprints somewhere on their surface. These fingerprints have been used to prove without doubt that certain paintings are the work of Leonardo.

Leonardo wrote in a strange way. He wrote his lines from right to left, and each letter was reversed. This is called 'mirror writing' because viewed in a mirror it looks quite normal.

human bodies, water, plants and animals. He kept notes of his observations in secret back-to-front 'mirror' writing.

Leonardo worked as an engineer for Italian nobles and for the French king. He designed forts and canals. The canals had locks so that boats could travel up and down hills. Leonardo also drew ideas for things long before they were invented. His drawings include a helicopter, a flying machine and a machine gun.

Leonardo was interested in many other things, including music and architecture. He was also a good musician and singer.

Leopard

Leopards are large, wild cats just a bit smaller than LIONS. They live in Africa and southern Asia. Most leopards are spotted like jaguars, but some are nearly black. These are called panthers.

Leopards are very fierce, strong and agile hunters. They catch and eat antelopes, goats, dogs and sometimes people. They often hunt from trees, lying in wait on a branch. If they cannot eat all their catch at once, they may haul the carcass high up into a tree. This is to stop lazier hunters such as lions or hyenas from stealing it.

▼ *Although they are fierce hunters, female leopards are good mothers and take great care of their young until they can fend for themselves.*

Lesotho

The kingdom of Lesotho is a small country completely surrounded by South Africa. Most of the people farm maize, wheat and sorghum, or raise sheep, goats and cattle. Nearly half of Lesotho's adults work in South Africa's mines, industries and farms. Lesotho, once called Basutoland, became a British protectorate in 1868. It gained its independence in 1966. The capital is Maseru.

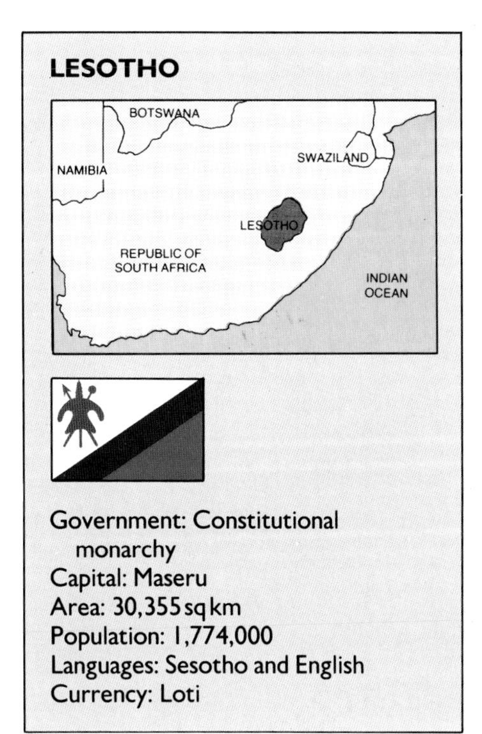

Liberia

Liberia is one of the oldest independent African countries. It has never been controlled by a European country. Liberia was founded in 1822 as a home for freed slaves from the United States. It is on the west coast and is less than half the size of the United Kingdom. It is easy to register ships in Liberia, so many countries do so there. Iron ore is Liberia's chief export. The capital is Monrovia. More than half the country's people became refugees as the result of a civil war that ended in 1991.

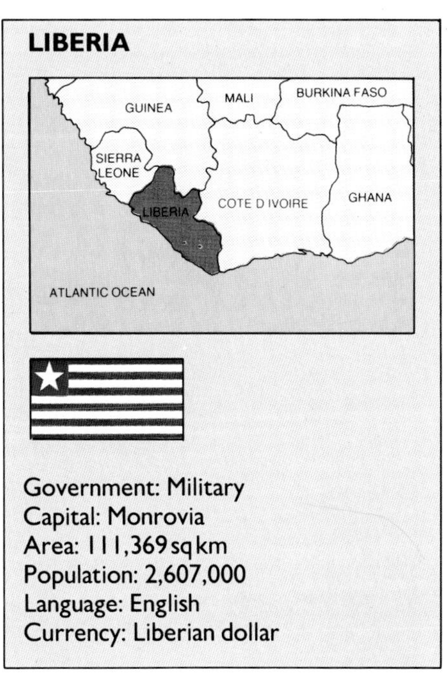

Libya

Libya is a large country in North AFRICA. It is more than three times the size of France, but very few people live there. This is because most of Libya lies in the SAHARA desert.

◀ *The Libyan port of Tripoli, on the Mediterranean, used to be called Medina. Its long history as a trading city dates back to biblical times.*

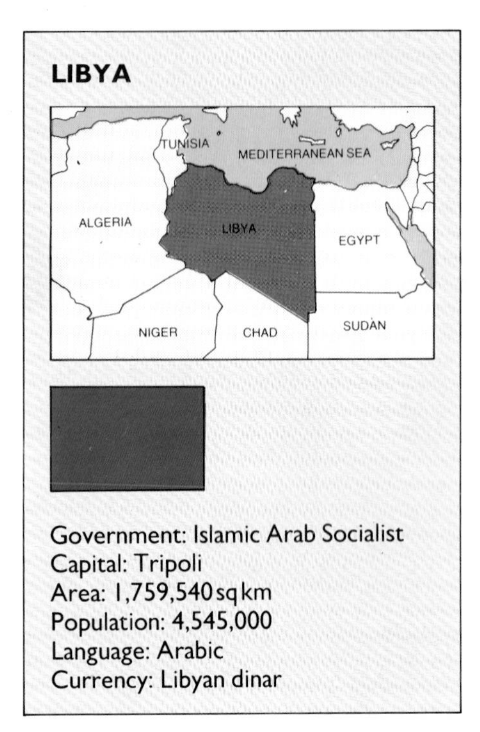

Government: Islamic Arab Socialist
Capital: Tripoli
Area: 1,759,540 sq km
Population: 4,545,000
Language: Arabic
Currency: Libyan dinar

Most Libyans are ARABS who farm the land. Libya is also rich in oil. The country became part of the Turkish Ottoman Empire in the 1500s, and was a colony of Italy from 1912 to the end of World War II. It became an independent monarchy in 1952 as the United Kingdom of Libya. In 1969 army officers overthrew the king and took control, and Colonel Muammar al-Qaddafi became head of the government. Since that time Qaddafi has led a revolution in Libyan life and many nations have accused him of interfering in other countries' affairs.

Lichen

A lichen is a simple PLANT. It has no roots, leaves or flowers. Some lichens grow as crusty patches on rocks, trees or walls. They grow very slowly. A patch no larger than your hand may be hundreds of years old. Other lichens grow as shrubby tufts. Lichens can live in places that are too bare, dry, cold or hot for any other plant.

► *A lichen is actually made up of two plants – a fungus and an alga – growing together. Reindeer moss, though called a moss, is actually a lichen.*

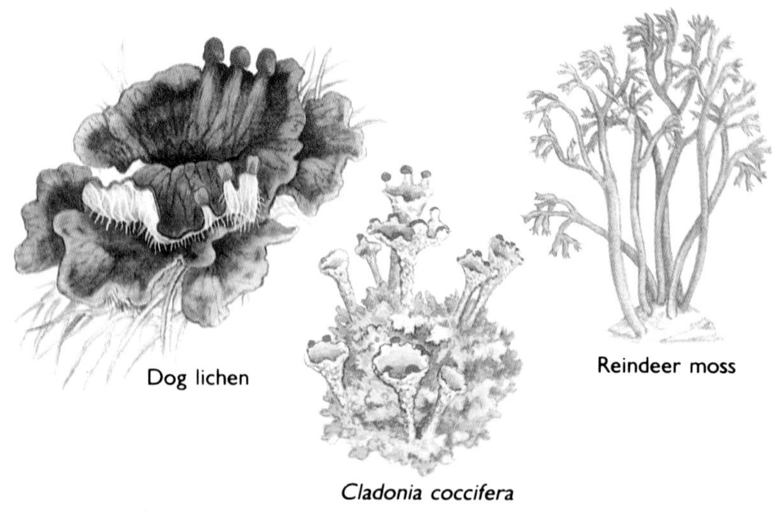

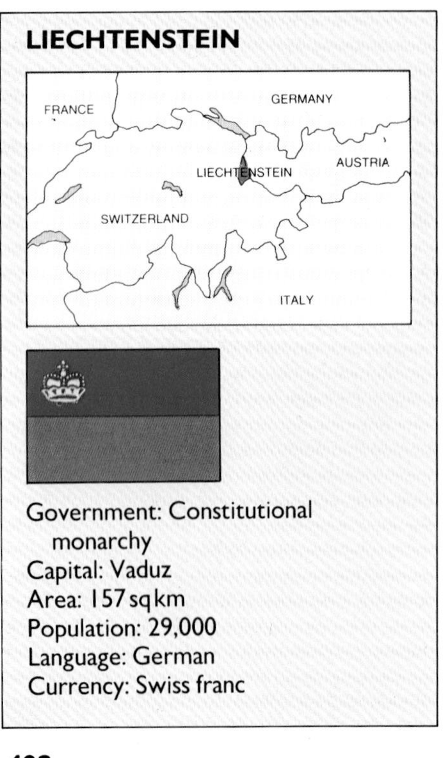

Government: Constitutional monarchy
Capital: Vaduz
Area: 157 sq km
Population: 29,000
Language: German
Currency: Swiss franc

Liechtenstein

Liechtenstein is one of the smallest countries in the world. It lies between Switzerland and Austria in the Alps. Liechtenstein is a prosperous country. Many international companies have their headquarters there. Tourism brings money into Liechtenstein. Switzerland runs the postal and telephone systems and the two countries use the same money. Liechtenstein is ruled by a prince.

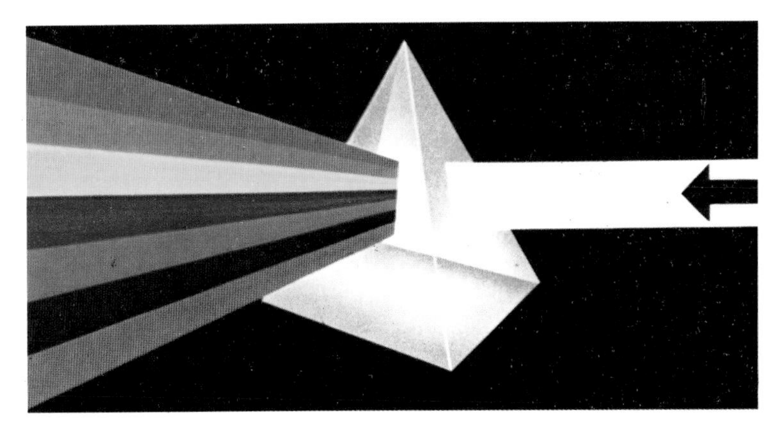

◀ *A prism splits white light into a spectrum of colours. When the sun shines through rain, the raindrops act as a prism to make a rainbow.*

Light

Light is a kind of ENERGY that we can see. Some objects—stars, lamps, certain chemicals—produce light. Most things do not produce light. We can see them only because they reflect light. For example, we can see the Moon and planets such as Venus and Jupiter in the sky only because they reflect light from the Sun.

Sunlight is the brightest light we normally see. Summer sunlight can be as bright as 10,000 candles burning close enough to touch. Bright sunlight seems white, but it is really made up of the colours of the RAINBOW. Isaac NEWTON showed this. He made a sunbeam shine through a specially shaped chunk of glass called a prism. Red, orange, yellow, green, blue, indigo and violet rays of light came out of the prism.

The prism had split the sunbeam into separate beams, each with its own *wavelength*. This is easy to understand if you think of light travelling in waves. The distance between the tops of the waves is the wavelength. We see each wavelength as a different colour. Long waves are red, short waves are violet, and wavelengths in between show up as all the other colours in the rainbow.

Light travels very fast, more than 300,000 km each second. Even so, it takes eight minutes for the light from the Sun to reach Earth, a distance of 150 million kilometres. A light year is the total distance a beam of light travels in one year—9,470,000,000,000 kilometres. Scientists use light years to measure how far away STARS are. Some are millions of light years away.

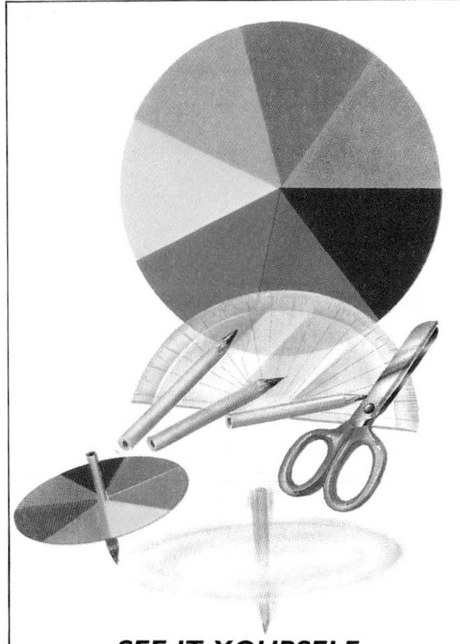

SEE IT YOURSELF

Here is a way to show that white light is made up of the seven colours of the rainbow. Cut a disc from card and divide it into seven equal sections. Colour each section as shown. Make a small hole in the middle of the disc and push a sharp pencil or stick through. Spin the disc quickly. What do you see?

▼ *When light rays travel through different substances, in this case air and water, they are bent so the image looks distorted.*

► *Lightning is caused by a build-up of static electricity in the atmosphere. When it discharges it causes a flash and the bang we know as thunder.*

Lightning

Lightning is ELECTRICITY that you can see. It is a sudden flow of electric current between two clouds, between a cloud and the ground, or between two parts of the cloud. There are three types of lightning. Streak lightning flashes in a single line from cloud to earth. Forked lightning happens when the lightning divides to find the quickest way to earth. Sheet lightning happens inside a cloud and lights up the sky, like the flashbulb on a camera.

▼ *Lincoln was the 16th president of the United States. He was shot just five days after the Civil War ended by John Wilkes Booth, an actor who supported the defeated South.*

Lincoln, Abraham

Abraham Lincoln (1809–1865) was president of the United States from 1861 to 1865. He had little schooling, but studied law on his own.

In 1854 a law was passed allowing people in new western territories to own slaves. In 1856 Lincoln joined the new, anti-slavery Republican Party and was elected president in 1860. Abraham Lincoln started a second term of office in 1865, just as he was trying to unite the nation at the end of the CIVIL WAR. But on April 14, 1865, on a visit to Ford's Theater in Washington, D.C., he was shot dead by John Wilkes Booth, an actor.

▼ *Lindbergh's historic flight across the Atlantic inspired many other pioneering aviators.*

Lindbergh, Charles

Charles Augustus Lindbergh (1902–1974) was an American pilot who became the first man to fly the Atlantic Ocean alone. His single-engine aircraft,

Spirit of St. Louis, left New York on May 20, 1927. He landed on May 21 in Paris, $33\frac{1}{2}$ hours later, after flying about 5600km non-stop. Lindbergh's flight made him an international hero. Later he helped to plan air tours to South America and over the Atlantic Ocean.

▲ *When lions are not hunting, they spend long periods resting to conserve their energy. Lions used to roam wild over southern Europe, India and Africa. Now they live only in South and East Africa and a tiny part of India.*

Lion

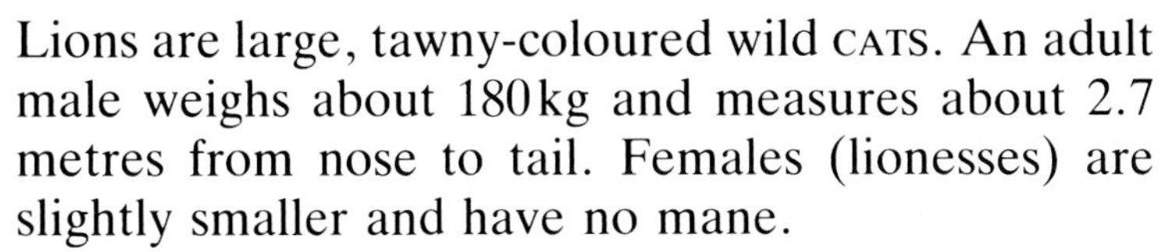

Lions are large, tawny-coloured wild CATS. An adult male weighs about 180kg and measures about 2.7 metres from nose to tail. Females (lionesses) are slightly smaller and have no mane.

Lions usually live in groups called prides. A pride has one male, several females and all their cubs. Lions often hunt as a team. No other big cats seem to do this. They hunt mainly antelope and zebra. Lionesses do most of the hunting.

Many lions today lead protected lives on nature reserves where they are safe from humans.

Liquid

A liquid can flow and change its shape. Liquids include water, milk, mercury and oil. When liquid is poured into a container, it takes the shape of the container but its volume remains the same. As a liquid gets hotter, the atoms or molecules in it move faster. They begin to leave the liquid. A GAS is formed. At the boiling point, the liquid boils and in time all of it turns into gas.

▼ *The elastic 'skin' on the surface of pond water is strong enough to prevent pond skaters from sinking. The 'skin' is caused by the force called 'surface tension'.*

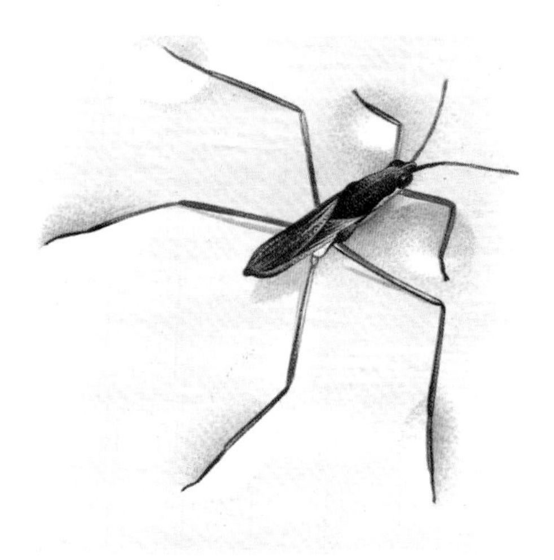

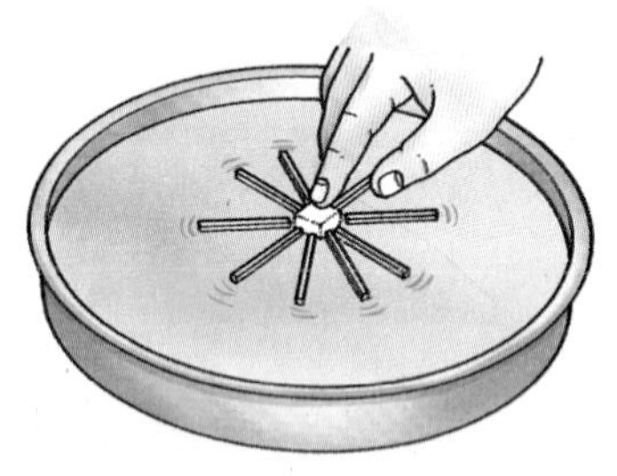

SEE IT YOURSELF

The surface of water is held together by a force called 'surface tension' which makes water appear to have a thin, elastic 'skin' all over it. To show that sugar breaks this 'skin', lay some matches carefully on the surface of a bowl of water as shown. Now dip a lump of sugar in the middle. The sugar absorbs some of the water and a small current of water flows towards the sugar, pulling the matches with it.

When a liquid gets colder, the atoms or molecules in it slow down. At the freezing point, they settle into rows and the liquid becomes a solid.

Lister, Joseph

Joseph Lister (1827–1912) was an English surgeon who found a way to stop his patients from dying of infection after operations. He used antiseptics to kill germs on surgeons' hands and instruments.

Lithuania *See* Baltic States.

Liver

Your liver is a flat, triangular organ tucked under your right ribs. It is larger than your stomach. The liver is a kind of chemical factory and storage cupboard. It produces the digestive juice that burns up the fat you eat. It makes the PROTEINS used in blood. It gets rid of any poisonous substances in the blood or changes them so that they are harmless. Minerals and VITAMINS are stored in the liver.

Livingstone, David

David Livingstone (1813–1873) was a Scottish doctor and missionary who explored much of southern and central AFRICA. He travelled to spread CHRISTIANITY and to help stop traders selling Africans into SLAVERY.

David Livingstone's parents were very poor. They and seven children lived in a single room at the top of a tenement building on the banks of the river Clyde. At the age of ten, young David had to go to work in a cotton mill, and with part of his first week's wages he bought himself a Latin grammar!

► *Stanley and Livingstone explored the Rusizi River in their search for the source of the Nile. They discovered that the river flowed into, and not out of, Lake Tanganyika and so could not be the Nile.*

Livingstone made three great journeys between 1841 and 1873. He crossed Africa, discovered the Victoria Falls and searched for the source of the river NILE.

In 1869, people feared that he had got lost or was dead. In 1871, a newspaper reporter, Henry Morton Stanley, found him at Lake Tanganyika. Both men continued their explorations, but Livingstone fell ill and died as he travelled.

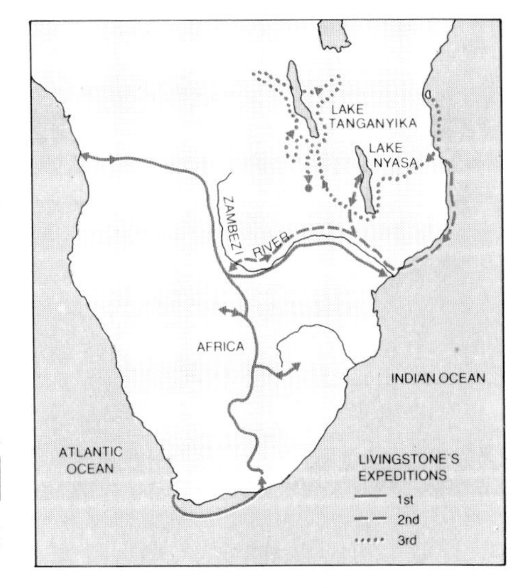

▲ *When Livingstone first went to Africa, it was largely uncharted. During his 32 years there, he became one of the greatest African explorers.*

Lizard

Lizards are REPTILES with dry, scaly skins and long tails. Most have four legs but some have none. These look like snakes. Some lizards are born live like MAMMALS, but most of them hatch from eggs.

There are about 3000 kinds of lizard. Most live in hot countries. Lizards that live in cooler places spend the winter in HIBERNATION. Lizards mainly eat insects.

Most lizards are only a few centimetres long, but the Komodo dragon of Indonesia is longer and heavier than a man.

▼ *Three different lizards. The Australian thorny devil has strong spines which have replaced the scaly skin found on other lizards. Komodo dragons can grow up to 3m long and eat wild pigs, young buffaloes and small deer. The European slow worm is not a worm at all, but a lizard. It has smooth, slippery scales and no limbs.*

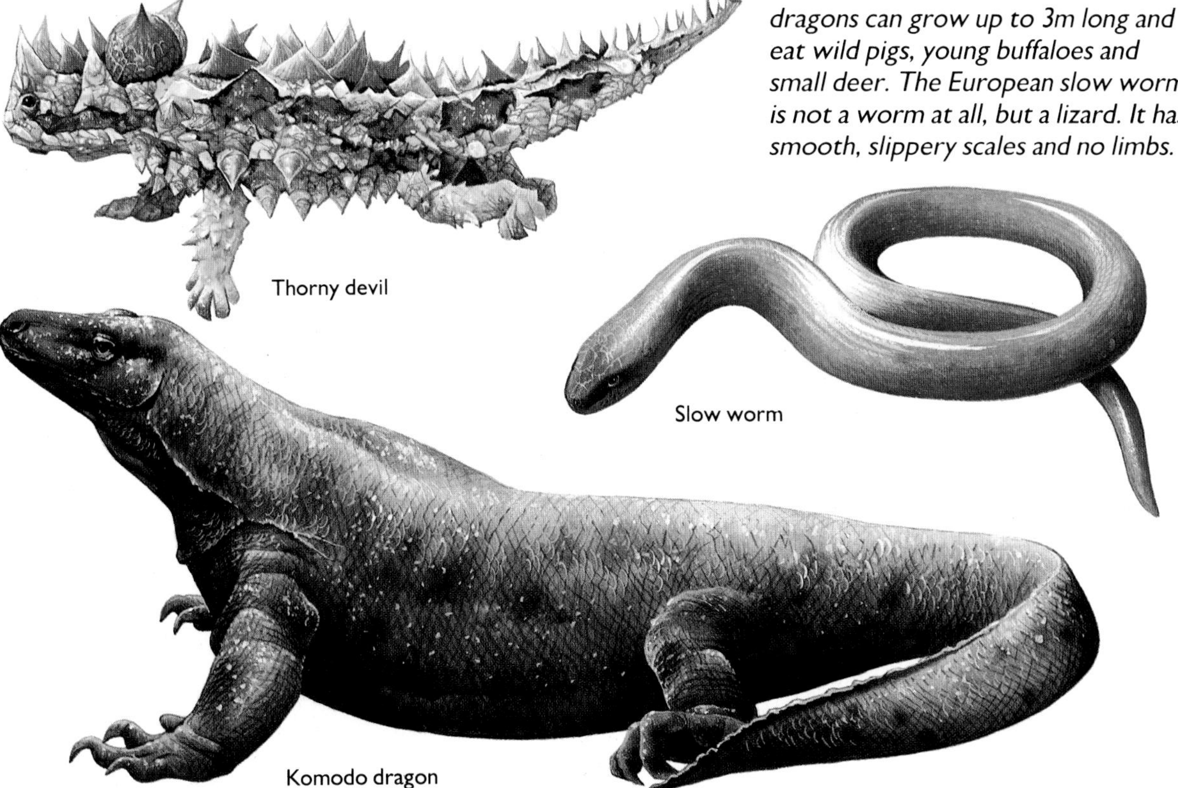

▲ *Llamas are hardy animals, well-adapted to the harsh conditions of the Andes mountains.*

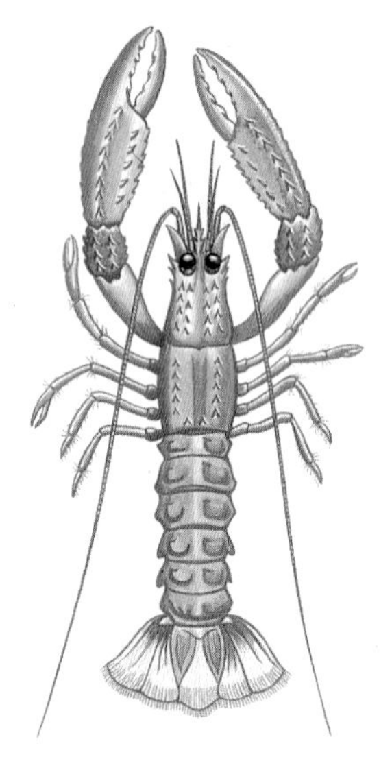

▲ *Norway lobsters are more familiar to us as scampi or Dublin Bay prawns.*

The earliest locks and keys were large wooden instruments. One can get some idea of the size of the keys from an Old Testament reference in Isaiah: 'And I will place on his shoulder the key of the house of David.' This probably shows how people carried their keys.

Llama

The llama belongs to the camel family, but has no hump. It stands about 1·5 metres high at the shoulder and may weigh twice as much as a man. Long, thick hair keeps it warm on the cold slopes of the Andes Mountains in South America, where it lives.

All llamas come from wild ancestors who were tamed at least 4500 years ago by the INCAS. Today, South American Indians still use llamas to carry heavy loads. They make clothes and ropes from the llama's wool and candles from its fat.

Lobster

Lobsters are CRUSTACEANS. They are related to shrimps and CRABS. One kind of lobster can weigh up to 20 kg. The lobster's body has a hard SHELL. It has four pairs of legs for walking and a pair of huge claws for grabbing food. When a lobster is afraid it tucks its tail under its body. This drives water forwards and pushes the lobster backwards to escape.

Lobsters hide among rocks on the sea bed. They feed on live and dead animals. A female lobster can lay thousands of eggs.

Lock and Key

There are two main kinds of lock. In the simplest kind, when the key is turned a piece of metal, called a bolt, moves out and fits into a slot. The key has a few notches that have to fit with similar notches in the lock. The Yale lock was invented in 1860. In it the key can turn a cylinder when all the little pins in the lock are pushed to the right height by the notches on the key.

Locust

Locusts are GRASSHOPPERS that sometimes breed in huge numbers. They fly far across land and sea to find new feeding places. A big swarm may have hundreds of thousands of locusts. When they land, the locusts eat everything green. Swarms of locusts have destroyed many farms in warm lands.

Locusts swarm and fly away only when they become too numerous and crowded. Farmers try to kill the young locusts before they are able to fly.

London

London is the capital of the UNITED KINGDOM. It has about seven million people. The river THAMES runs through London.

People from all over the world visit London to see Buckingham Palace, the Houses of PARLIAMENT, Westminster Abbey and the Tower of London. There are many museums, theatres and parks in London, as well as offices and factories.

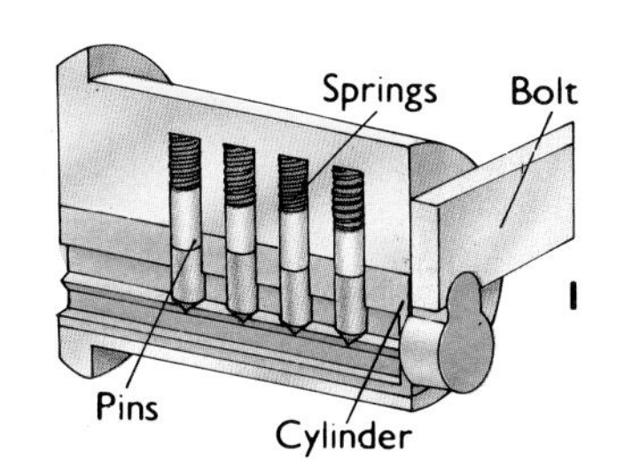

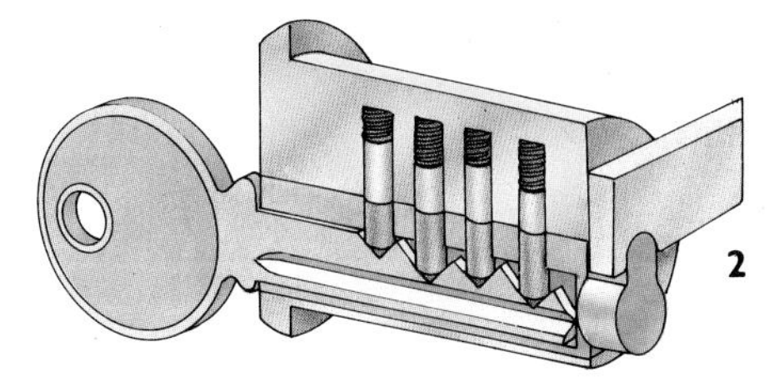

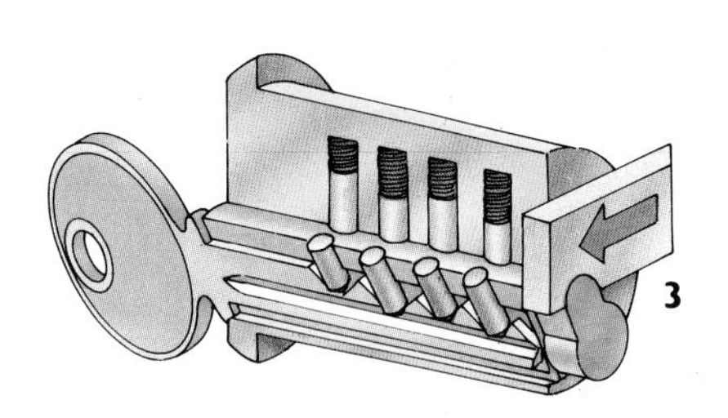

▲ *In a Yale lock there are many combinations possible for the heights of the pins. Before the key is inserted, all the pins are level and held in place by springs (1). The key slides into the lock and its jagged edge pushes the pins to different heights (2). When the right key is used, the pins are pushed to the heights that will allow the cylinder to be turned, opening the lock (3).*

◀ *The Tower of London has been the site of a fortification since Roman days, and has seen some of the most turbulent moments of British history.*

London began as a Roman settlement called *Londinium*. The PLAGUE came to London in the 1600s, followed by the Great Fire of 1666. The city was badly bombed in WORLD WAR II.

London is very slowly sinking into its foundations and the level of the river Thames is slowly rising. As a result, extra-high tides could flood a large part of London. To prevent this happening, a great barrier has been built across the Thames at Woolwich. If very high tides happen, the barrier can be raised and London will be safe.

Los Angeles

Los Angeles is the second-largest city in the UNITED STATES. More than 14 million people live in the Los Angeles area. The city lies in the sunny countryside of California. On one side of Los Angeles is the Pacific Ocean. Behind it are the San Gabriel Mountains.

There are thousands of factories and a big port in Los Angeles. Visitors go to see Disneyland and Hollywood. Los Angeles makes more cinema and television films than any other city in the world.

► *The air pollution in Los Angeles is so severe it can actually be seen. The smog forms a thick haze over the city, particularly in hot, dry weather.*

▼ *When sound is recorded it is turned into electrical signals. The loudspeaker turns these signals back into sound waves that we can hear. The signals are fed to a coil that is attached to a plastic cone and positioned between the poles of a circular magnet. The signals cause the coil to vibrate, which vibrates the plastic cone. The cone produces sound.*

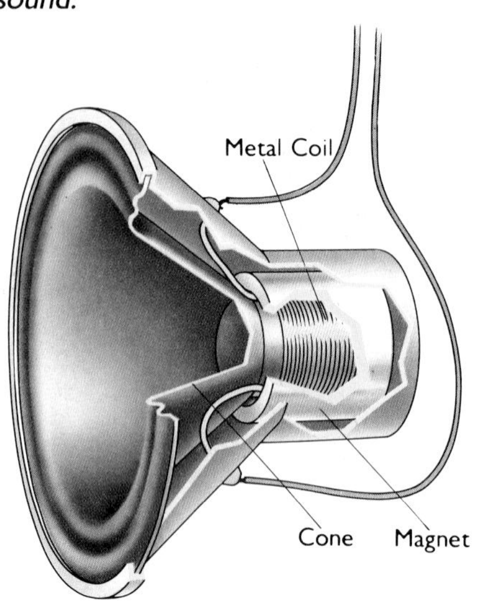

Loudspeaker

A loudspeaker turns electric signals into SOUND waves. The sounds that we hear on RADIO, TELEVISION, record players and tape recorders all come from loudspeakers.

A moving coil loudspeaker has a cone fixed to a wire coil. Inside the coil is a magnet. Electric signals flow through the coil. The signals make the coil move to and fro. The tiny movements of the coil make the cone shake, or vibrate. Air around the cone also starts to vibrate. These air vibrations reach our ears and we hear sounds.

◀ *Louis XVI was king of France at the time of the French Revolution. He was executed on 21st January 1793, after a two-month trial.*

Louis (French kings)

Eighteen French kings were called Louis.

The first was Louis I (778–840). Louis IX (1214–1270) led two CRUSADES. Louis XI (1423–1483) won power and land from his nobles. Louis XIII (1601–1643) made the French kings very powerful. Louis XIV (1638–1715) ruled for 72 years. He built a great palace at VERSAILLES. All the French nobles had to live in his palace. Louis XVI (1754–1793) was beheaded after the FRENCH REVOLUTION.

▲ *Louis XIV was called the Sun King because of the splendour of his court. His palace at Versailles was more like a small city than a home.*

Lung

Lungs are organs for BREATHING. People have lungs, and so do many animals. Lungs bring OXYGEN to the body from the AIR. They also remove waste carbon dioxide from the BLOOD.

Your lungs are two large, sponge-like masses in your chest. They fill with air and empty as you breathe in and out.

You breathe in air through the nose. The air flows down the windpipe, or *trachea*. Where the lungs begin, the trachea divides into two hollow branches called bronchial tubes, or *bronchi*. Each divides into smaller tubes called *bronchioles*. These end in cups called air sacs, or *alveoli*. This is where the lungs give oxygen to the blood and take away carbon dioxide.

Lungs need clean air. Smokers and people who live in smoky towns, or work in some kinds of dusty air, may get lung diseases.

▼ *The soft, fragile lungs are well protected inside the rib cage, which expands and contracts to allow for the movements of breathing.*

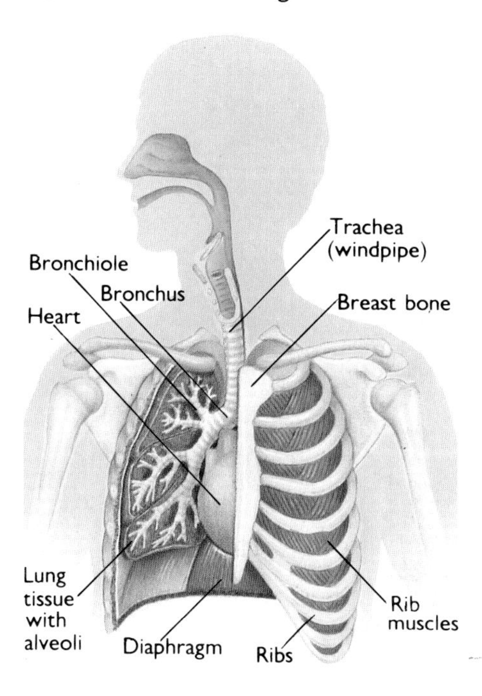

▲ *Luther made a list of 95 arguments against the Church's practice of selling pardons, and nailed them to a church door in Wittenberg.*

Luther, Martin

Martin Luther (1483–1546) was a German priest who quarrelled with the ROMAN CATHOLIC CHURCH. He started the Protestant REFORMATION.

Luther did not like the way priests forgave people's sins in return for money. He also believed that God's teachings lay in the BIBLE. The Bible was more important to Luther than what the POPES said.

Under Luther's leadership, a large number of Christians split away from the Roman Catholic Church.

LUXEMBOURG

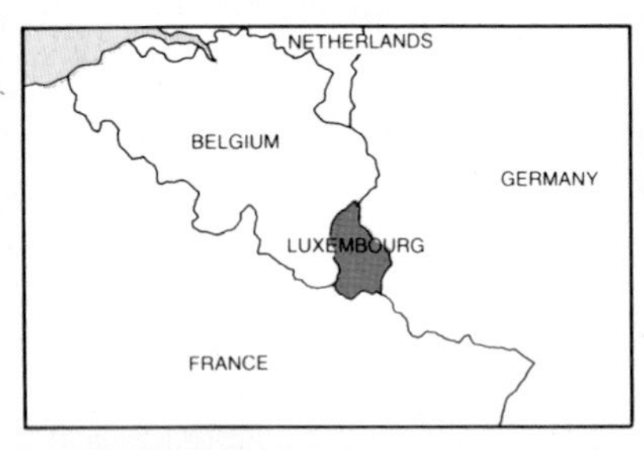

Government: Constitutional monarchy
Capital: Luxembourg
Area: 2586 sq km
Population: 373,000
Languages: French and Letzeburgesch
Currency: Luxembourg franc

Luxembourg

Luxembourg is one of the smallest countries in EUROPE. Around it are Belgium, France and Germany. Luxembourg has low mountains with large forests. There are farms in the hills. There are also iron mines and towns that make steel. The capital city has the same name as the country. The European PARLIAMENT has offices in the capital.

Luxembourg has less than half a million people. Their own language is Letzeburgesch, but many speak French or German. Luxembourg is in the EUROPEAN COMMUNITY.

Machine (Simple)

Some machines are very large and have many moving parts. Other machines are very simple. All the machines we see working around us are related to one or other of six simple machines. These machines were among people's oldest and most important inventions.

A machine is stronger than a person. It uses a greater *force*. When a force is used to move something, we can say that *work* is done. Machines make work easier. The *wedge*, for example, helps us to split things. A wedge hammered into a small crack in a tree trunk will split the trunk in two. Chisels, knives, nails and axes are all different forms of wedges.

The SCREW can pull things together or push them apart. With a screw jack, a man can quite easily lift a car weighing far more than himself. There are many kinds of *levers*. The simplest is a long pole, pivoted or balanced on a log and used to lift a heavy rock. The lever changes a small downward force into a bigger upward force.

The *inclined plane* makes it easier to raise heavy loads to higher levels. It is easier to pull a load up a slope than to lift it straight up. The PULLEY also makes lifting easier. A simple pulley is used in the winding mechanism that raises water from a well. A more complicated machine is the block and tackle, which has several sets of ropes and pulleys.

Probably the most important of all simple machines is the *wheel and axle*. This is used not only for moving loads, but also in all sorts of machines – such as clocks.

▼ *Machines make it easier for us to do work. When we operate them, we do a little work over a long distance so that the machine can do a lot of work over a short distance. For example, in the screw jack shown below, you have to turn the lower bar many times to raise the upper bar only a little, but this bar can raise a very great weight.*

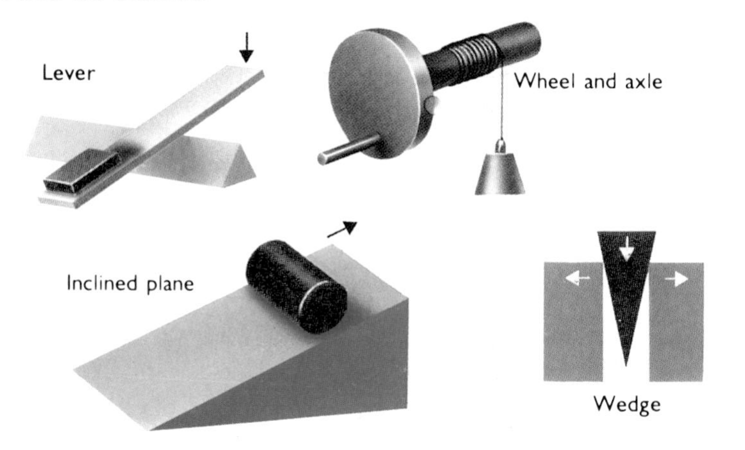

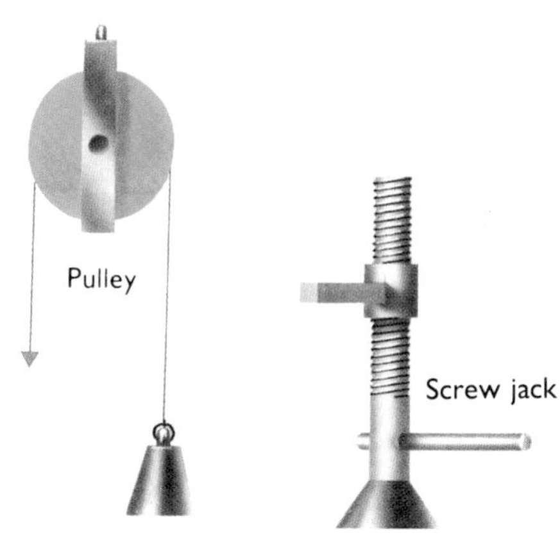

MADAGASCAR

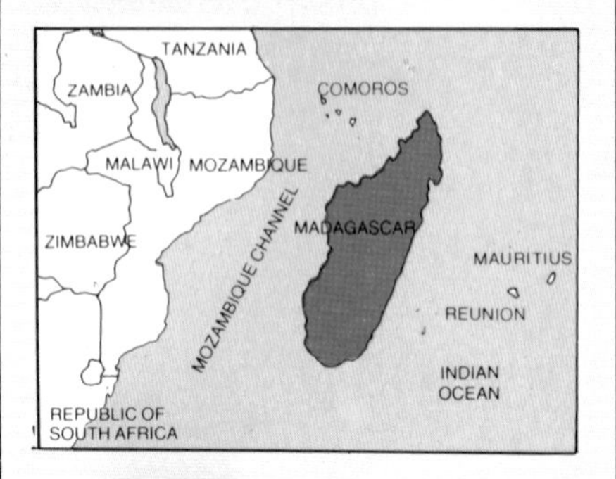

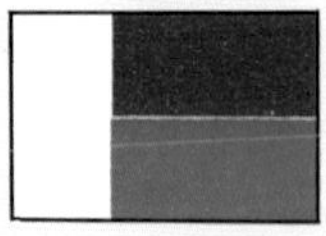

Government: Republic
Capital: Antananarivo
Area: 587,041 sq km
Population: 11,197,000
Languages: Malagasy and French
Currency: Malagasy franc

Madagascar

Madagascar is the fourth largest island in the world. It is in the Indian Ocean, off the east coast of Africa. The country of Madagascar has fertile coastal plains, a rugged central plateau and a warm, tropical climate. Coffee, rice, sugar and vanilla are among the leading crops.

Between the 800s and 1300s, Arab colonies were set up in Madagascar. In the 1800s the island came under French control. It gained independence from France in 1960. The government is socialist.

Madrid

Madrid is the capital city of SPAIN. It was chosen by King Philip II (1527–1598) as his capital because it was in the middle of the country. Madrid is a dry, windy city; cold in winter and hot in summer. It is the centre of Spanish life, and the seat of the country's parliament. It has many fine buildings, including the Prado, which has one of the finest collections of paintings in the world. More than 3,000,000 people live in Madrid, which is the centre of Spain's road and railway network.

Magellan set sail from Seville, Spain, on September 20, 1519. His expedition consisted of five ships and about 270 men of many nationalities. When the expedition reached Spain again on September 6, 1522 after its round-the-world voyage, only one ship was left. It had a crew of 17 Europeans and 4 East Indians picked up on the voyage.

Magellan, Ferdinand

Ferdinand Magellan (1480–1521) was a Portuguese sailor and explorer. In 1519 he sailed west from Spain, round Cape Horn and into the Pacific Ocean. Magellan was killed by natives in the Philippines. But one of his five ships returned safely to Spain, having completed the first voyage around the world.

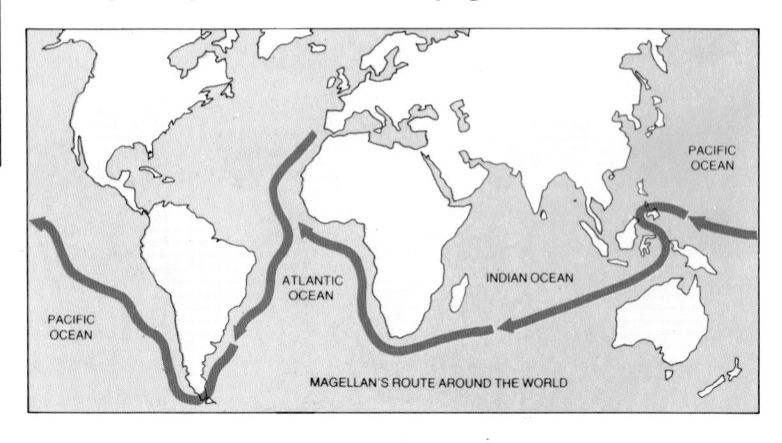

▶ *Magellan set out to find a new sea route to Asia, heading west and rounding the tip of South America.*

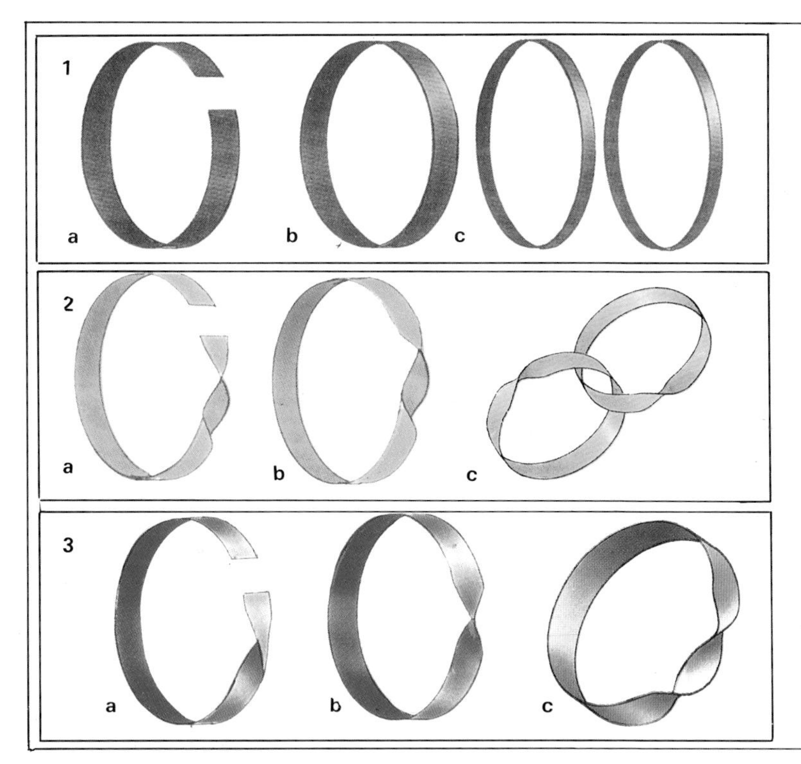

SEE IT YOURSELF

Here is a magic trick using three loops of paper. Take three strips of paper, each about a metre long and 5 cm wide. Take the first strip and glue the ends together to form a loop (1a and b). Do the same with the second strip, but give it a complete turn (turn it over and over again) before joining the ends (2a and b). With the third strip, turn one end over once before gluing (3a and b). Now cut the three strips down the centre. The first loop gives you two separate loops (1c). The second forms two linked loops (2c). The third becomes a single loop twice the size of the original (3c)! These magic loops were discovered by a famous German mathematician, Ferdinand Moebius, in 1858.

Magic

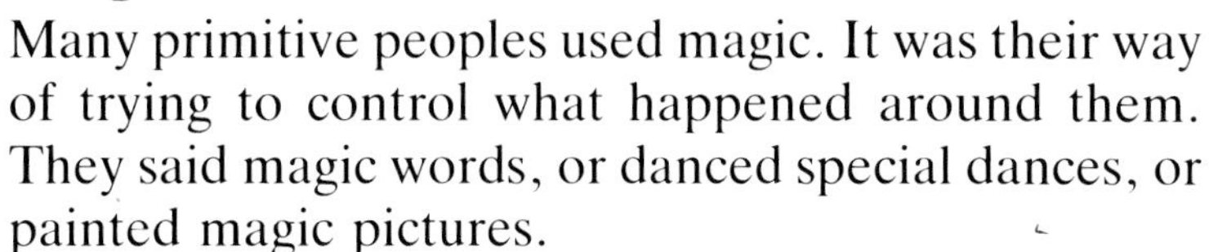

Many primitive peoples used magic. It was their way of trying to control what happened around them. They said magic words, or danced special dances, or painted magic pictures.

All through history people have believed that certain things (such as talismans or charms) or people (such as witches and sorcerers), have magical powers. Magic is often closely tied up with religion. But most people today think of magic as the conjuring tricks performed by magicians on television, in the theatre or at parties.

Magna Carta

The Magna Carta is a signed agreement, or charter, that was drawn up in England in the time of King JOHN. In those days, not even the great barons, or nobles, could argue with the king. This was accepted by everyone, providing the king governed the country fairly.

But King John was not a good ruler. He demanded extra taxes from the people and quarrelled with the barons. In 1215 the barons met and

▼ King John was forced to sign the Magna Carta by the rebel barons at Runnymede.

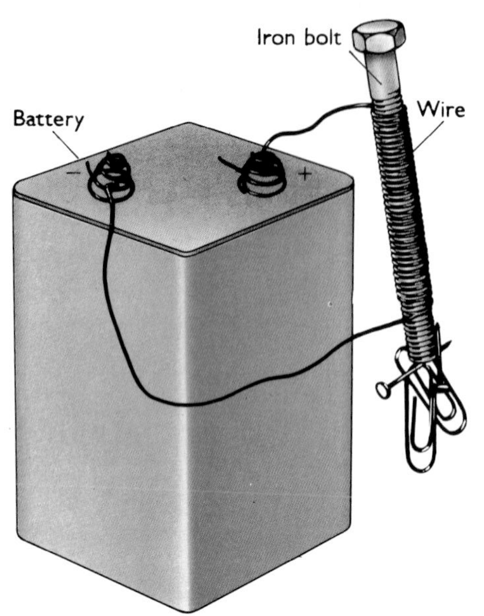

▲ *In an electromagnet, a metal that is not normally magnetic, such as an iron bolt, can be made so by passing an electric current through a coil of wire wrapped around it. As soon as the current is broken, the magnetic field ceases to exist.*

demanded that John sign the Magna Carta, or 'great charter'. This document marked the beginning of a new system of government in which the king had to rule according to the law.

Magnetism

A magnet attracts metals, particularly iron and steel. The Earth is a huge natural magnet. Invisible lines of magnetic force spread out round the planet, joining the North and South magnetic poles. We call this the Earth's *magnetic field*.

The needle in a COMPASS is a magnet. It always turns to face magnetic North. In ancient times people noticed that a kind of iron ore called a lodestone suspended from a string would always swing to point in the same direction. A lodestone is a natural magnet. Another name for it is magnetite.

An electromagnet is made by coiling wire round a metal core and passing electricity through the coil. Electromagnets can be made more powerful than ordinary magnets.

SEE IT YOURSELF

If you have two bar magnets you can show the shapes of force-fields around the magnets. Put one of the magnets under a piece of plain paper and sprinkle some iron filings on top (1). The filings show the lines of force running between the north and south poles of the magnet. Now do the same thing using the two magnets. You will see why a north pole attracts a south pole (2), and why two north poles or two south poles push each other apart (3).

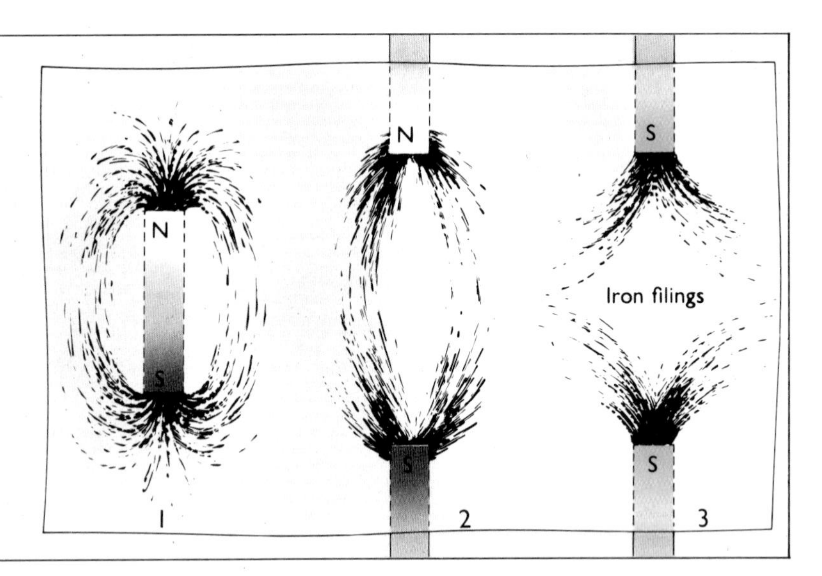

The word 'malaria' means 'bad air' in Italian. It was first called this because people thought that the disease was caused by gases from the swampy regions where many cases occur.

Malaria

Malaria is a common and deadly tropical disease. It is carried by the female *Anopheles* MOSQUITO, which can infect the humans it bites. Drugs are used to treat malaria. Scientists try to destroy the mosquitoes and the swamps in which the insects breed.

◀ *In Malawi, traditional methods of farming and the village way of life still exist.*

Malawi 

Malawi is a long, narrow country in eastern Africa. It is half the size of the United Kingdom. Most of Malawi's people live in small villages and grow their own food. Tobacco, tea and sugar are grown.

The explorer, David LIVINGSTONE, was the first European to come to the region of Malawi, in 1859. In 1891, Britain took over the territory and set up the Protectorate of Nyasaland. Independence was granted in 1964. The name was changed to Malawi, the name of the people who once lived there.

MALAWI

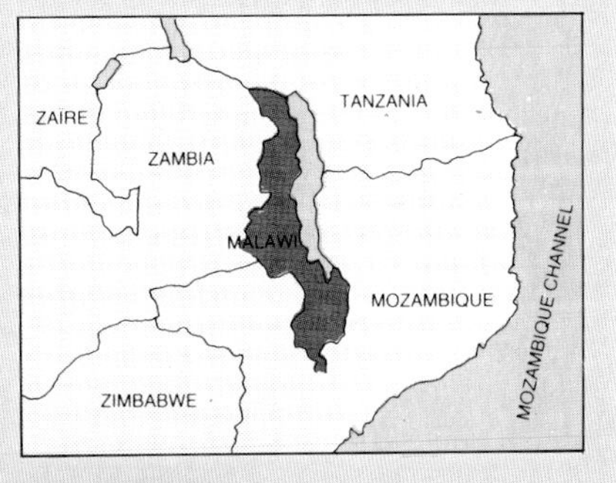

Government: Republic
Capital: Lilongwe
Area: 118,484 sq km
Population: 8,289,000
Languages: English and Chichewa
Currency: Kwacha

Malaysia 

Malaysia is a country in SOUTH-EAST ASIA. It is in two parts, West Malaysia on the Malay Peninsula, and East Malaysia, which is part of the island of Borneo. The capital, Kuala Lumpur, is in West Malaysia.

Malaysia has over 17,000,000 people, mostly Malays and Chinese. Its main exports are rubber, timber and tin.

Malaysia is a member of the Commonwealth. It is ruled by a sultan, who is head of state, and a prime minister, who is head of government.

MALAYSIA

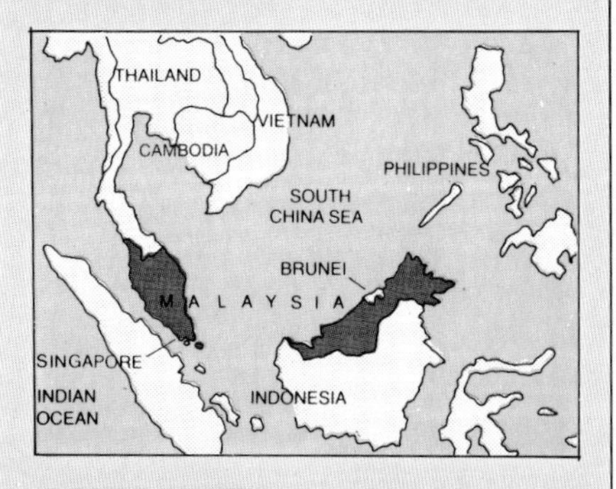

Government: Constitutional monarchy
Capital: Kuala Lumpur
Area: 329,749 sq km
Population: 17,861,000
Languages: Malay, English and Chinese
Currency: Ringgit

Maldives 

The Republic of Maldives is a chain of islands south-west of India in the Indian Ocean. Although there are about 2000 islands, the total area is much less

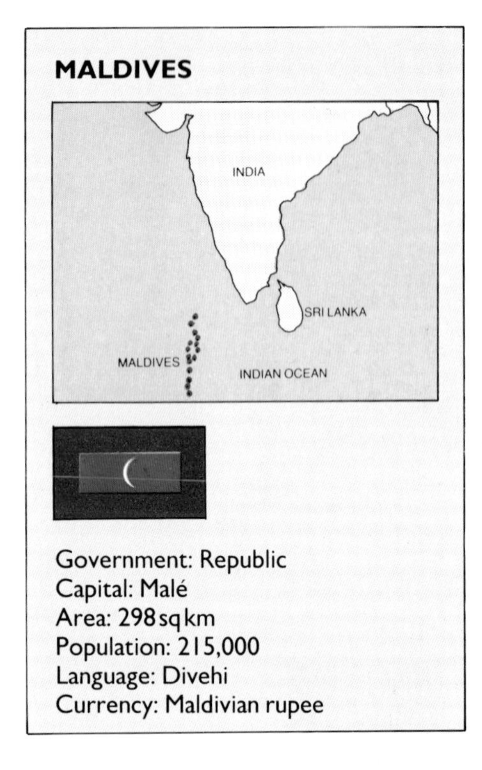

than that of London. The climate is damp and hot, with heavy rainfall. Most of the people make their living by fishing.

The islands became a British protectorate in 1887 and gained complete independence in 1965. The Maldives is one of the world's poorest countries.

Mali

The country of Mali is in north-west Africa. It is five times the size of the United Kingdom but has only an eighth of its population. A large part of the country is in the Sahara Desert.

In the 1800s Mali was occupied by the French, and achieved independence in 1960. Famine and drought have plagued the country.

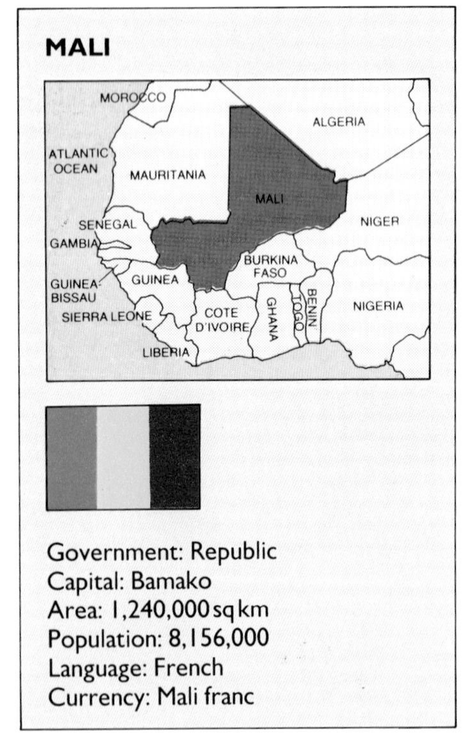

Malta

Malta is an island in the MEDITERRANEAN SEA. It lies south of Sicily. Since ancient times it has been a vital naval base, for it guards the Mediterranean trade routes to the East. For centuries Malta was ruled by the Knights of St John, but in 1813 it became British. During World War II, Malta survived heavy bombing raids and the whole island was awarded the George Cross medal.

▶ *Fishing boats at anchor in a harbour in Gozo. The Republic of Malta includes the island of Malta and its neighbouring island, Gozo.*

Since 1962 Malta has been self-governing. Today, it is a republic. The capital is Valletta, with its splendid Grand Harbour.

MALTA

Government: Republic
Capital: Valletta
Area: 316 sq km
Population: 358,000
Languages: Maltese and English
Currency: Maltese pound

Mammal

Mammals are not the largest group of animals on Earth. But they are the most intelligent and show a greater variety of forms than any other group of animals.

All mammals have warm blood and a bony skeleton. Many have hair or fur on their bodies to keep them warm. Female mammals give birth to live young, which they feed on milk from special glands in their bodies. Some mammals (such as mice) are born naked, blind and helpless. Others (such as deer) can run within hours of being born.

Mammals were the last great animal group to appear on Earth. They came long after fish, amphibians, reptiles and insects. When DINOSAURS ruled the Earth, millions of years ago, the only mammals were tiny creatures which looked like SHREWS. But after the dinosaurs died out, the mammals took over. During EVOLUTION, the mammals multiplied into many different forms which spread all over the world.

Scientists divide the mammals into three families.

▼ *The age of the mammals began in the Cenozoic era. These mammals of the early Cenozoic include the glider* Planetotherium *(far left), the plant-eater* Barylambda *(centre), the long-tailed* Plesiadapis *(top right) and* Taeniolabis *(bottom right). At bottom left is an early shrew.*

The most primitive mammals still lay eggs, like the reptiles and birds. There are only two left in this family, the echidna and the PLATYPUS. Then come the MARSUPIALS. These mammals give birth to tiny, half-developed young which have to be carried in their mother's pouch until they are big enough to look after themselves. The best known marsupial is the KANGAROO. Almost all the marsupials live in Australia.

The 'placental' mammals, the highest group of all, give birth to fully developed young. There are many different kinds, including flying mammals (BATS); gnawing animals or RODENTS; sea mammals (WHALES and DOLPHINS); and burrowing mammals (for example, MOLES). There are insect-eaters, plant-eaters and flesh-eaters. The flesh-eaters, or CARNIVORES, include the powerful CATS, WOLVES and BEARS. The most intelligent of all the mammals are the primates. This family includes MONKEYS, APES and HUMAN BEINGS.

EGG-LAYING MAMMALS

MARSUPIALS

PLACENTAL MAMMALS

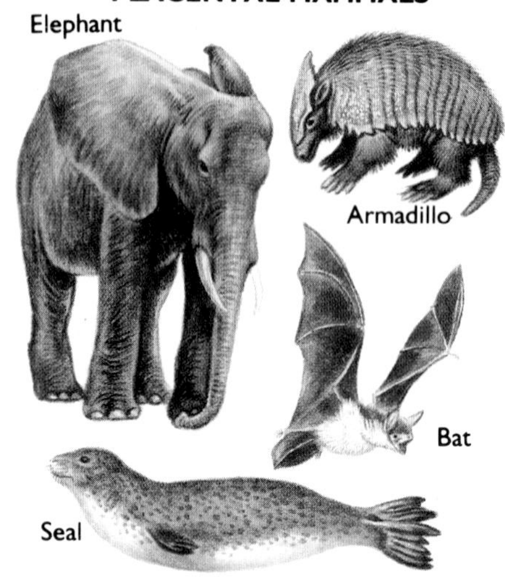

▲ *There are three families of mammals: egg-laying mammals, marsupials and placental mammals. The placental mammals are the most advanced group.*

Mammoth

During the ICE AGES, woolly mammoths roamed the plains of Europe and North America. They looked like shaggy-haired elephants, with long curling tusks. But they lived in much colder climates than the elephants of today.

▶ *Woolly mammoths developed from a more primitive creature called the Mastodon, which was also the ancestor of the modern elephant.*

Mammoths lived together in herds, feeding on plants, grass and leaves. Their enemies included the fierce sabre-toothed tiger, wolves and also CAVE DWELLERS, who hunted mammoths for food. Sometimes a group of hunters drove a mammoth into a pit, where it could be killed with spears.

The frozen bodies of mammoths have been dug up by scientists in the icy tundra of Siberia. Mammoth remains have also been found in tar pits in California. The last mammoths died out about 30,000 years ago.

About 40 mammoths have been found frozen into the Arctic ice of Alaska and Siberia. The meat of these great creatures was so fresh that it could be eaten by dogs after more than 30,000 years.

Maoris

The Maoris are the native people of NEW ZEALAND. These well-built, brown-skinned people came in canoes from Pacific islands to New Zealand in the 1300s. The Maoris were fierce warriors who fought with clubs made of bone or greenstone (a kind of jade). They fought many battles against the white people who first came to New Zealand. This war did not end until 1865, and there were some outbreaks of fighting for years afterwards.

The Maoris were very skilful at weaving, dancing, and, above all, carving. Maori carving is full of decoration. Every inch of the surface of their work is covered with curves, scrolls and spirals. Their tools were made from greenstone, and they carved

▲ *Tikis are an important part of Maori art and culture. This tiki, carved from jade, was worn for protection against the ghosts of still-born children.*

The Maoris developed ceremonial *haka* dances. The *haka* has become known in many countries since 1889, when the New Zealand rugby union team, the All Blacks, began the tradition of performing a *haka* before each game.

◀ *Maoris of the older generation mix traditional and modern ways of life. This woman wears a tiki and has tattoos on her chin.*

▲ *Mao was chairman of the Communist Party in China for 27 years, and brought about many radical changes in culture and economics.*

greenstone, a kind of jade, to make little figure ornaments called *tikis*. Tattooing was also an important part of Maori art.

Today, Maoris play an important part in the life of New Zealand. Their population is increasing at a faster rate than that of non-Maoris.

Mao Tse-tung (Mao Zedong)

Mao Tse-tung (1893–1976) was a great Chinese leader. He was the son of a farmer and trained to be a teacher. In 1921 he helped to form the Chinese Communist Party and fought against the Chinese Nationalists under Chiang Kai-shek. In 1934 he led 90,000 Communists on a 368-day march through China to escape Nationalist forces. This feat was called the Long March. When Mao Tse-tung and the Communist armies beat the Nationalists he became head of the Chinese government in 1949. He wanted China to become as rich as America, but many of his plans for his country did not work. He resigned from his job as head of government in 1959 but carried on as head of the Chinese Communists. He had many arguments with the Russian Communists. Mao also wrote books about guerrilla warfare, and poetry.

After Mao's death, China's new leaders criticized his rule and gradually brought in a more Western-looking policy.

▼ *Early maps and globes show what a mysterious place the world once was. A lot of guess-work went into mapmaking in years gone by.*

Map and Chart

We need maps and charts to help us find our way about. There are different kinds of maps. Some show countries, towns, roads and railways. These are *political* maps. *Physical* maps show natural features such as mountains, plains, rivers and lakes. The shape of features such as mountains is shown by colours or by contour lines.

Maps are drawn to different *scales*. The scale of some maps is so big that you might be able to find your house on one. The scale of other maps is very small so that we can even squeeze the whole world onto one page of an atlas. On a small-scale map, 2 cm on the map might represent 200 km, or

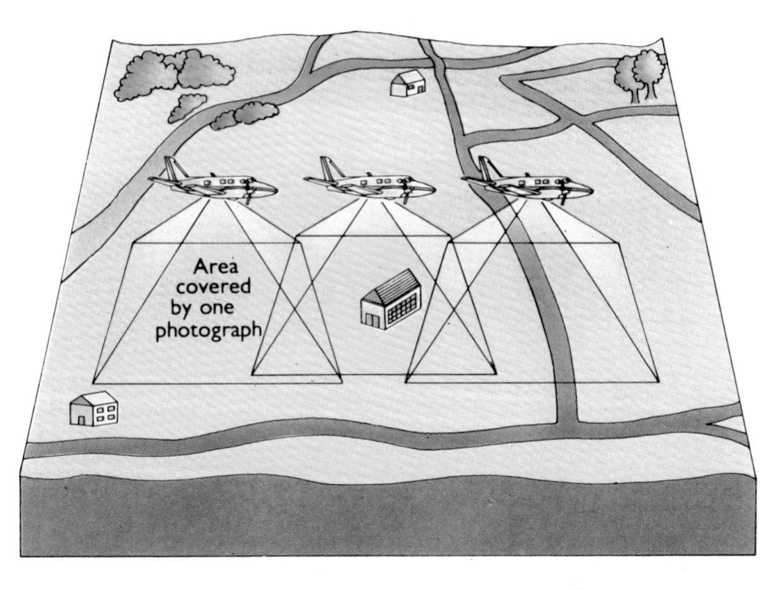

◀ *Today, aerial photographs are used to make accurate maps. The pictures are taken from a plane flying at a constant height. Each photo overlaps the next slightly, so no detail is lost.*

200,000 m, for example, on the ground.

Charts are maps of the sea. They tell sailors about lighthouses, rocks, channels and the depth of water in various places.

Marathon Race

The Marathon is a very hard long-distance race of 42·19 km (26 miles 385 yards). It has been run in the OLYMPIC GAMES since 1896. It was named after a Greek soldier's run from the town of Marathon to Athens in 490 BC to bring news of a Greek victory over the Persians. In 1908 there was a famous finish to the Olympic Marathon. At the end of the race a small Italian, Dorando Pietri, staggered into the stadium in the lead. He collapsed twice in the last 100 metres and had to be helped over the finishing line. He was disqualified because of this, but everyone remembers this as Dorando's Marathon.

▲ *Pheidippides was the soldier who ran with the news of Greek victory after the battle of Marathon.*

The official distance for the marathon is 26 miles 385 yards. The reason for this strange distance is that the British Olympic committee decided in 1908 to start the race from the royal castle at Windsor and finish in front of the royal box in the stadium in London. This was measured at 26 miles 385 yards, a distance that has remained standard ever since.

Marble

Marble is a rock that is formed when limestone is squeezed and made very hot inside the Earth. Pure marble is white, but most of the rock has other substances in it which give it lots of colours. If a piece of marble is broken, the broken faces sparkle like fine sugar. (The word marble means 'sparkling'.)

Marble has long been used for making statues as

▲ *Marble cut from a quarry (right) can be used to make beautiful patterns in a floor (left). The many different colours of marble are caused by impurities present when the rock was formed.*

well as for building. It is easy to shape and takes a high polish. The most famous marble for sculpture comes from quarries at Carrara in Italy. It is very white and has a very fine grain.

Marconi, Guglielmo

Guglielmo Marconi (1874–1937) was the man who, most people say, invented RADIO. His parents were rich Italians. When he was only 20 he managed to make an electric bell ring in one corner of a room, set off by radio waves sent out from the other corner. Soon he was sending radio signals over longer and longer distances. In 1901 he sent the first message across the Atlantic. In 1924 he sent signals across the world to Australia.

Marconi shared the Nobel Prize for physics in 1909 and was honoured throughout the world.

▲ *Marconi left Italy to continue his experiments in England because he did not get enough encouragement from the Italian government.*

Marco Polo *See* Polo, Marco

Margarine

This is a food like butter. It is made from vegetable FATS and OILS. VITAMINS are usually added to make it nearly as nourishing as butter. Margarine was invented in 1867 by a French chemist called Mège-Mouries. He won a prize offered by the French government for finding a cheap substitute for butter. Many people now eat margarine and similar spreads because they are low in unhealthy fats.

Marie Antoinette

Marie Antoinette (1755–1793) was the Austrian-born wife of LOUIS XVI of France. A beautiful and vivacious young woman, she found her husband dull and boring, and hated her duties as queen. Instead she spent money lavishly and cared little for the world outside the royal palace at Versailles. She became a symbol to the poor people of France of all they hated about the royal court. When the FRENCH REVOLUTION broke out in 1789, the king and queen were taken to Paris by force. They were executed on the guillotine in 1793.

▲ *Through her unthinkingly lavish spending, Marie Antoinette made the poor people of France hate her. She showed great courage at her trial, but was condemned to death and executed in October 1793.*

Mars (God)

Mars was one of the oldest and most important of the Roman gods. He was the son of Jupiter and Juno and became the god of war. His son, Romulus, was supposed to have been the founder of ROME. The temples and festivals of Mars were important to the Romans. The month of March was named after him. It was the first month in the Roman year.

Mars (Planet)

The planet Mars is only about half the size of the Earth. It takes about two years to travel around the Sun. The surface of Mars has huge volcanoes and great gorges, far bigger than those on Earth. Most of Mars is covered with loose rocks, scattered over a dusty red surface. This is why Mars is called the 'Red Planet'. It has a North Pole and a South Pole, both covered with snow or frost.

Seen through a telescope, the red surface of Mars is criss-crossed by thin grey lines. Some early astronomers thought that these lines were canals which had been dug by intelligent beings. They said these canals had been dug to irrigate the soil, since Mars has very little water. But space probes to Mars in 1965, 1969 and 1976 found no trace of the canals.

MARS FACTS

Average distance from Sun: 228 million km
Nearest distance from Earth: 78 million km
Temperature on sunlit side: 0 degrees C
Temperature on dark side: −170 degrees C
Diameter across equator: 6794 km
Atmosphere: Carbon dioxide
Number of moons: 2
Length of day: 24 hours 37 minutes
Length of year: 687 Earth days

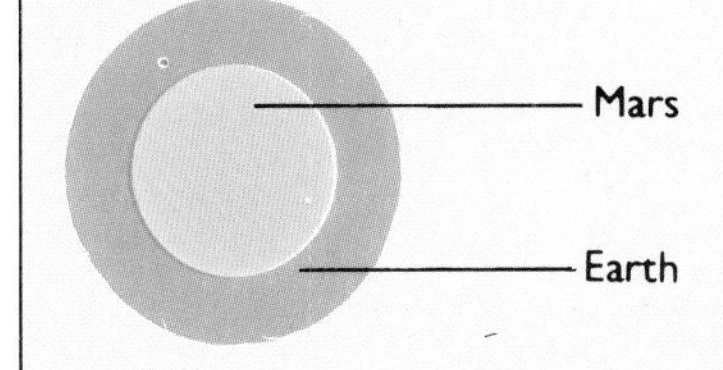

▶ *The dusty, red surface of Mars shows no trace of life. Viking space probes to the planet appear finally to have put an end to any ideas that there could be alien beings living there.*

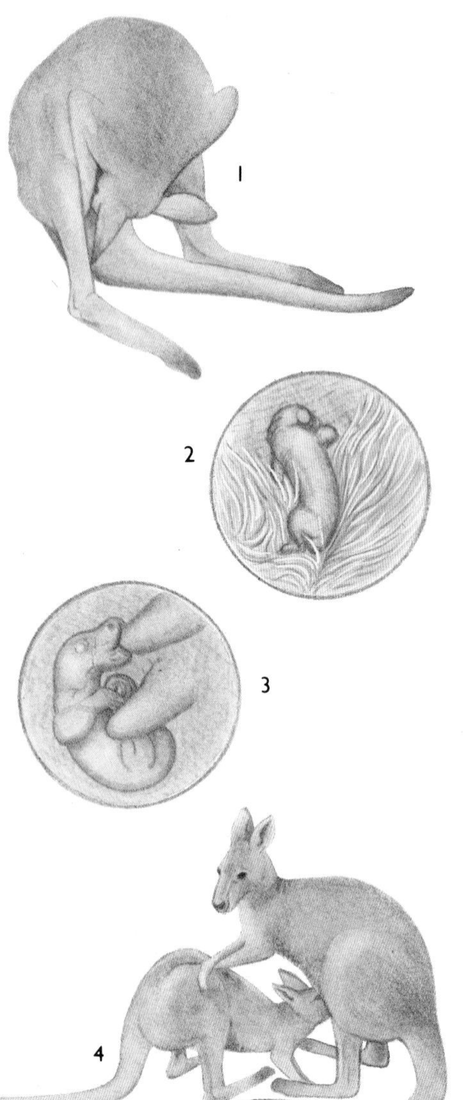

▼ *The kangaroo, like other marsupials, gives birth to its young before they are fully formed: (1) Before the birth, the female cleans her pouch and the fur around it. When the baby kangaroo is born, it crawls through the fur to the pouch (2). It attaches itself to one of the teats (3), and stays in the pouch for about 190 days until it is fully developed (4).*

The American Viking spacecraft landed on Mars and took samples of the planet's soil, but it was unable to find any kind of life on Mars.

The planet has two tiny moons – Phobos and Deimos. Phobos, the larger of the two, is only about 24 km across.

Because Mars has a smaller mass than the Earth, things on its surface weigh only about 40 per cent of what they would weigh on Earth. A day on Mars is about the same length as an Earth day.

Marsupial

Marsupials are MAMMALS with pouches – animals such as KANGAROOS, WALLABIES, BANDICOOTS, KOALAS and OPOSSUMS. They all live in Australia, except the American opossum. A newly-born marsupial is very tiny. It crawls into its mother's pouch and stays there, feeding on her milk, until it can look after itself.

Martial Arts

The martial arts are various kinds of combat that come from the Far East. They include judo, karate and aikido, all from Japan; and kung-fu, from China.

Judo, meaning 'easy way', is probably the most

popular. It originally came from jujitsu, a violent practice that could maim or kill. Today judo is a safe sport practised by men, women and children, and has been an Olympic sport since 1964. It is used in many parts of the world for self-defence. A trained student of judo can quickly unbalance an opponent and throw him or her to the ground.

In karate and kung-fu, the hands, elbows and feet are used as weapons. Aikido, like judo, makes use of the opponent's strength to unbalance him. Kendo, another form of self-defence, is a kind of fencing using sticks instead of swords.

▲ *Although the martial arts were developed as methods of combat, they are now widely enjoyed as sport. Kendo, judo and karate are all safe if practised with proper supervision.*

Marx, Karl

Karl Marx (1818–1883) was a political thinker and writer whose ideas brought about great social and political changes. Marx was born in Germany and his ideas were the starting point of COMMUNISM. He believed that people who own property, the capitalist class, keep those who work for them down so the owners can become richer. He also thought that the workers would one day rise against the capitalists and take control. Marx's ideas later inspired communist revolutions all over the world, notably the Russian Revolution.

◄ *Karl Marx (right), with Lenin (left) and Engels, heroes of communism. Between them Marx and Engels developed the ideas that inspired Lenin to found the communist state in Russia.*

▲ *Mary I's attempts to make England a Roman Catholic country were foiled by Elizabeth I when she succeeded as queen.*

▼ *Mary, Queen of Scots' determination to become Queen of England led to her execution in February 1587.*

Mary I, Queen

Mary I (1516–1558) was the daughter of King HENRY VIII and his first wife, Catherine of Aragon. Mary became queen after Edward VI died in 1553. Her marriage to Philip II of Spain involved England in European wars. Mary's attempts to restore Roman Catholicism led to the execution of many Protestants. This is why she was given the nick-name, 'Bloody Mary'. She was succeeded by her half-sister, ELIZABETH I.

Mary, Queen of Scots

Mary, Queen of Scots (1542–1587) was the last Roman Catholic ruler of SCOTLAND. The daughter of James V of Scotland, she was educated in France, and did not return to Scotland until she was 19. By that time she thought of herself as more French and Catholic than Scottish and Protestant.

Mary was the heir to the English throne after her Protestant cousin ELIZABETH I. In 1567 Mary was forced to give up the Scottish throne. Later she was imprisoned for 20 years in England. People said she was plotting against Queen Elizabeth. She was executed on the queen's orders in 1587.

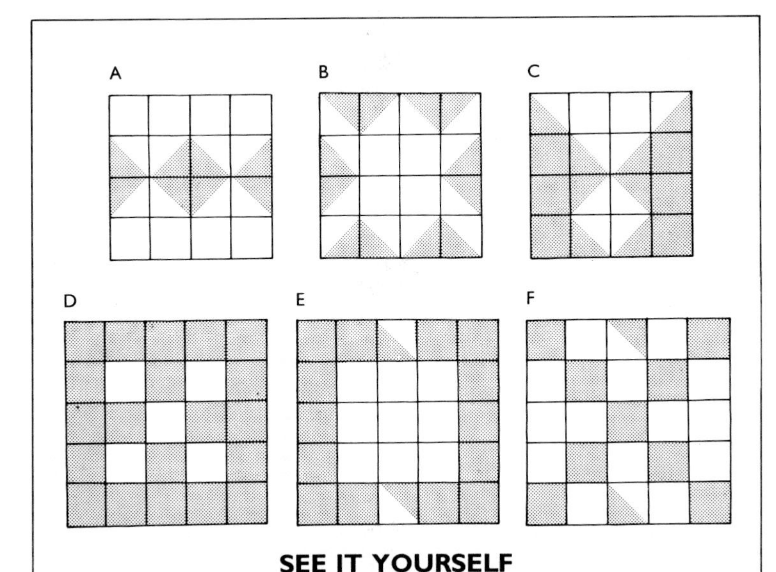

SEE IT YOURSELF

You can work out fractions by counting squares and half squares. What fraction of each grid has been coloured? The answers are at the bottom of the page.

Some numbers are magic! Take the quite ordinary-looking number 142857, for example. Try multiplying it by 2. You get 285714. The same digits in the same order, but moved along. Now try multiplying our magic number by 3, by 4, by 5 and by 6. (A calculator will make it easier.) See what happens! And there's more. Try dividing it by 2 and by 5.

Mathematics

We all use mathematics every day. We add up the coins in our pockets to find out how much money we have. We look at a clock and work out how much time we have left before going somewhere. In every business people are constantly using some kind of mathematics; often, nowadays, with the help of calculators and computers. The branch of mathematics that deals with numbers is called arithmetic. ALGEBRA uses symbols such as *x* and *y* instead of numbers. GEOMETRY deals with lines, angles and shapes such as triangles and squares.

Matter

Everything you can see and touch is matter – and so are some things you can't. Matter is anything that has *volume* – that takes up space. Scientists say that matter has *mass*, the amount of matter in something. The mass of something always remains the same. The pull of gravity gives you weight, but your weight can change. If you go to the Moon you will weigh only a sixth as much as you do on Earth. But your mass will still be the same.

Matter can be grouped into three main forms –

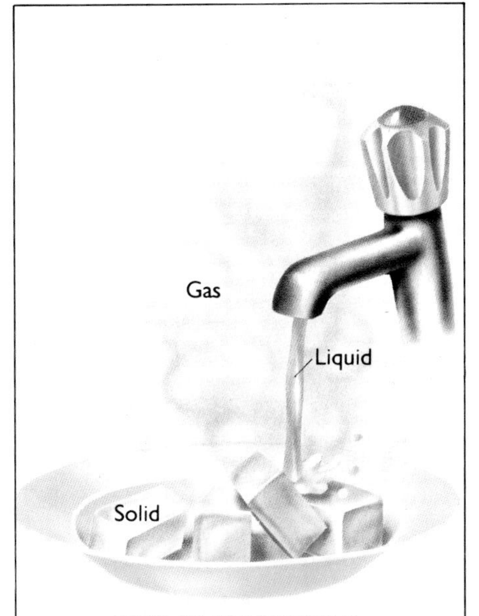

SEE IT YOURSELF

Every substance is either a solid, a liquid or a gas at room temperature. But if the temperature changes, the substance can change its state. The picture shows the three states of water. Hot water in its normal liquid state is being poured onto ice cubes, which are water in its frozen solid state. Rising above the melting ice is steam, which is water in its gaseous state.

A = 1/4; B = 3/8; C = 5/8; D = 4/5; E = 3/5; F = 2/5.

solid, liquid and gas. This book is solid, the water that comes from the tap is liquid, and the air that we breathe is a gas. The solid, liquid and gas forms are called the three 'states' of matter.

But nearly all matter can exist in all three forms. If air is made cold enough it becomes a liquid. A gas can be turned into a solid by cooling it. Solids such as iron can be turned into liquids by heating them. In the Sun, iron and other kinds of matter exist as gases because it is so hot.

Mauritania

Mauritania is an Islamic republic on the west coast of Africa. It is a very large country, but much of it is desert, where nomads keep cattle, sheep and goats. The valley of the Senegal River and the southern coastal areas are the only fertile regions.

Mauritania became a French protectorate in 1903 and became independent in 1960. There is often a threat of famine.

MAURITANIA

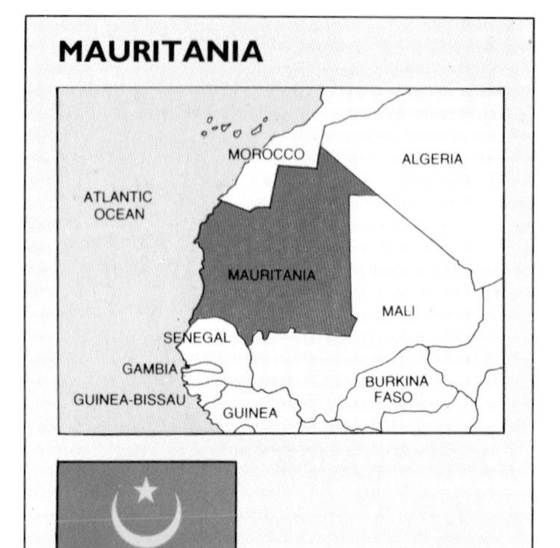

Government: Military republic
Capital: Nouakchott
Area: 1,030,700 sq km
Population: 2,025,000
Languages: French and Arabic
Currency: Ouguiya

Mauritius

Mauritius is a small island country in the Indian Ocean. Most of the island is surrounded by coral reefs. The island is thought to be the peak of an ancient volcano. Mauritius is one of the most densely populated places in the world. There are about 500 people for every square kilometre of the island. The chief crops are sugar cane and tea. Tourism is a growing industry.

MAURITIUS

MOZAMBIQUE
MADAGASCAR
MAURITIUS
REUNION
INDIAN OCEAN

Government: Constitutional monarchy
Capital: Port Louis
Area: 2085 sq km
Population: 1,075,000
Languages: English and French
Currency: Rupee

► *A view of the Rempart Mountains on the island of Mauritius, which has many volcanic hills.*

◀ *Mayan temples are huge and imposing buildings, showing skill in architecture and engineering.*

▼ *A Mayan carving in serpentine, a kind of rock, showing the god Tlaloc.*

Maya

The Maya Indians first lived in Central America in the AD 400s. They grew maize and sweet potatoes and kept pet dogs. Later they built cities of stone, with richly decorated palaces, temples, pyramids and observatories. Even today, many of these wonderful buildings are still standing, hidden in the jungle. The Maya were also skilled in astronomy and mathematics, and they had an advanced kind of writing.

The Maya people did not have any metals until very late in their history. They built with only stone tools, and had no knowledge of the wheel. Their lives were controlled by religion. They worshipped a sun god, rain gods, soil gods and a moon goddess who looked after women.

Measure *See* Weights and Measures

Mecca

Mecca is the Holy City of the Muslims, and MUHAMMAD's birthplace. It is in Saudi Arabia. In the centre of Mecca is the Great Mosque, and in the mosque's courtyard is the Ka'aba, which houses the sacred 'Black Stone'. Muslims believe it was given to Abraham by the archangel Gabriel. This stone is kissed by pilgrims to Mecca.

▼ *An old painting showing Abdul-Muttalib, Muhammad's grandfather, opening the Ka'aba door.*

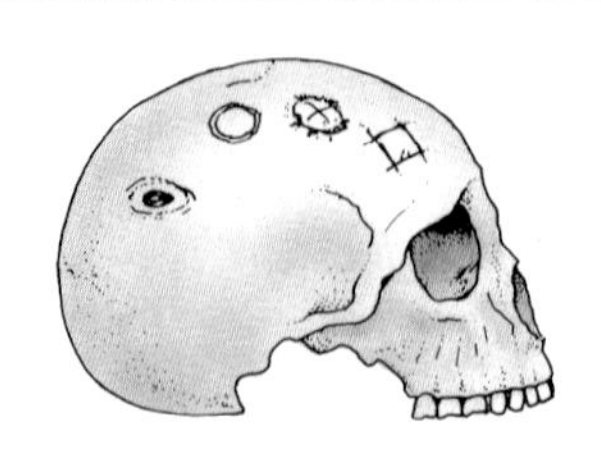

▲ Prehistoric men removed pieces from the skull to release evil spirits.

▲ In Indian medicine, a steam pipe, called a Nadi-Svedi, was used from about 400BC to help wounds heal quickly.

► The irong lung was invented in 1876 to keep patients alive when their lungs failed to work.

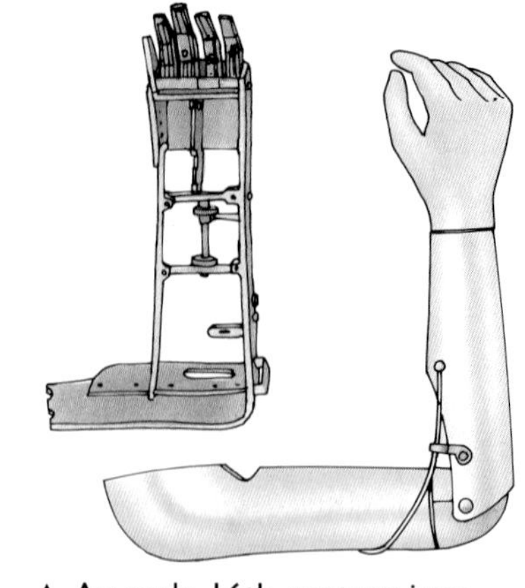

▲ An early 16th century iron hand (left) and a modern arm and hand (right).

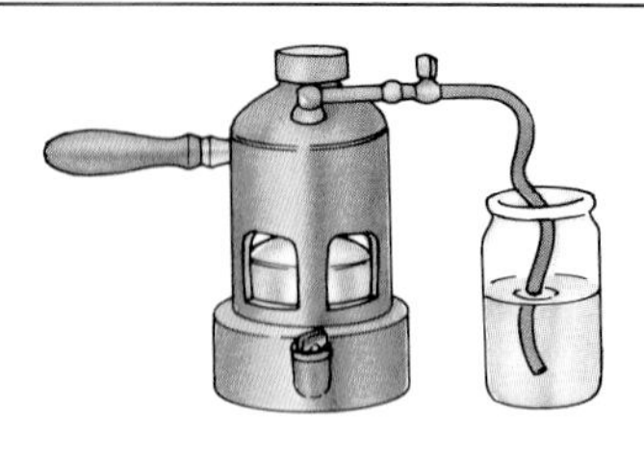

▲ Joseph Lister's carbolic acid sprayer was used to sterilize operating theatres.

▼ This kidney machine helps patients with kidney failure.

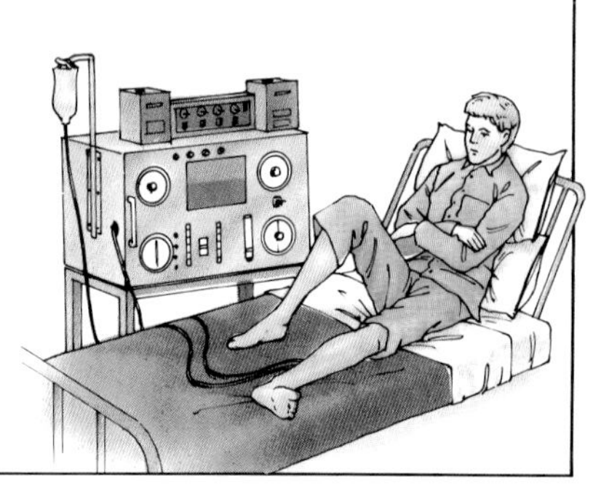

▲ *Medicine has made huge advances from superstition and magic to the high-tech hospitals of today.*

ADVANCES IN MEDICINE

1590 **Microscope** – Zacharias Janssen
1593 **Thermometer** – Galileo
1628 **Blood circulation** – William Harvey
1796 **Vaccination** – Edward Jenner
1846 **Anaesthetic** – William Morton
1865 **Antiseptic surgery** – Joseph Lister
1865 **Germs cause disease** – Louis Pasteur
1895 **X-rays** – William Roentgen
1898 **Radium** – Pierre and Marie Curie
1922 **Insulin for diabetes** – Frederick Banting and Charles Best
1928 **Penicillin** – Alexander Fleming
1954 **Polio vaccine** – Jonas Salk
1967 **Heart transplant** – Christiaan Barnard

Medicine

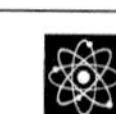

When we first think of the word 'medicine' perhaps we think about all the tablets, powders, pills and liquids people take when they are not feeling well. But medicine also means the science of healing. It has taken a long time for medicine to become truly scientific.

In the early days doctors relied mostly on magic cures, prayers and charms. But in the last few hundred years medicine has advanced faster than in all of human history. The development of anaesthetics in the last century was a vital step forward in progress in surgery. And in this century progress has been fastest of all. Scientists have found out about VITAMINS; they have made all kinds of wonder drugs like penicillin; they have almost wiped out DISEASES such as tuberculosis and smallpox; they are finding out more and more about mental illness; and they can now give people spare parts for many parts of their bodies when these organs go wrong. But perhaps the most important area of a doctor's job is still *diagnosis*, finding out what is wrong with a patient by studying the symptoms.

Mediterranean Sea

The Mediterranean is a large sea surrounded by three continents – Africa, Europe and Asia. It flows out into the Atlantic Ocean through the narrow Strait of GIBRALTAR. It is also joined to the Black Sea by a narrow strait, or passage.

In ancient times the Mediterranean was more important than it is now. In fact, it was the centre of the Western world for a long time. The Phoenicians were a seafaring people who travelled around the Mediterranean from about 2500 BC. Then the Greeks and Romans sailed the sea. The Romans were in control of the whole Mediterranean for nearly 500 years. They even called it *Mare Nostrum*, Latin for 'our sea'.

The SUEZ CANAL was opened in 1869. It cuts across Egypt, joining the Mediterranean to the RED SEA. The canal was very useful because it shortened the distance by sea between Europe and the East. It is still used by cargo ships.

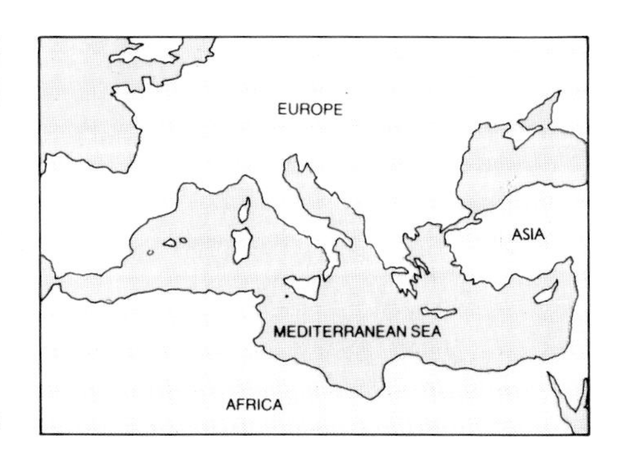

▼ *A 16th century map of the port of Genoa, in Italy. The Mediterranean has long been of vital importance to trade and commerce, and thriving towns grew up around its natural ports.*

▲ *Mendel's important findings were not believed at first. It was some years before his laws were generally accepted.*

Melbourne

Melbourne is the capital of the state of Victoria and the second largest city in AUSTRALIA. It has nearly three million people. This fine city lies at the mouth of the Yarra River on Port Phillip Bay. Melbourne's port is one of the biggest in Australia. It handles both overseas shipping and shipping to other states. Melbourne was the capital of Australia from 1901 to 1927, when Canberra became the capital.

Mendel, Gregor

Gregor Mendel (1822–1884) was an Austrian priest who became famous for his work on heredity. Heredity is the passing on of things such as eye colour, skin colour and mental ability from parents to their children.

Mendel grew up on a farm, where he became interested in plants. When he entered a monastery he began growing peas. He noticed that when he planted the seeds of tall pea plants, only tall pea plants grew. Then he tried crossing tall peas with short peas by taking pollen from one and putting it in the other. He found that again he had only tall plants. But when he crossed these new mixed tall plants with each other, three-quarters of the new plants were tall and one quarter were short. Mendel had found out that things like the tallness or shortness are controlled by tiny *genes*, passed on from each parent. Mendel also showed that some genes are stronger than other genes.

▼ *The god Mercury was supposed to look after writers, athletes, merchants, travellers, and thieves and vagabonds. As well as being the messenger of the gods, he was a bringer of good luck and a protector of flocks and shepherds.*

Mercury (God)

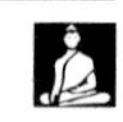

Mercury was a Roman god who was the same as the Greek god Hermes. He was the messenger of the gods and is usually shown as a young man with winged sandals and wearing a winged hat.

Mercury (Metal)

Mercury, or quicksilver, is the only metal that is a liquid at ordinary temperatures. When mercury is poured onto a table it forms little bead-like drops.

Most metals dissolve in mercury to make *amalgams*, used as fillings for teeth. Mercury is also used in THERMOMETERS and BAROMETERS.

Mercury (Planet)

The planet Mercury is one of the smallest planets in the SOLAR SYSTEM, and the closest to the Sun. A day on Mercury lasts 59 of our days. During the long daylight hours it is so hot that lead would melt. During the long night it grows unbelievably cold. Little was known about Mercury's surface until the space probe Mariner 10 passed within 800 km of the planet. It showed Mercury to have a thin atmosphere and big craters like those on the Moon.

Mercury travels very fast through space – at between 37 and 56 km per second. This great speed and its nearness to the Sun give it the shortest year of all the planets (a year is the time it takes a planet to go once round the Sun). Mercury's year lasts only 88 of our Earth days.

▲ *Drops of mercury look like little round beads. This is because of the attraction between mercury's molecules.*

MERCURY FACTS

Average distance from Sun: 58 million km
Nearest distance from Earth: 45 million km
Temperature on sunlit side: 350 degrees C
Temperature on dark side: −170 degrees C
Diameter across equator: 4878 km
Atmosphere: Almost none
Number of moons: 0
Length of day: 59 Earth days
Length of year: 88 Earth days

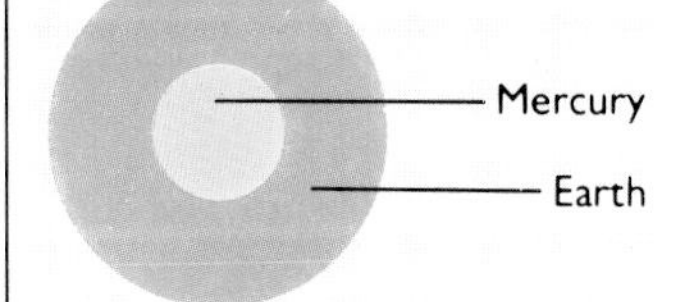

◀ *The Mariner 10 space probe passed Mercury three times in 1974 and 1975. It discovered that Mercury has a huge iron core, probably about three-quarters of the size of the planet.*

▲ *In legends, mermaids often lured ships onto the rocks. Seeing a mermaid was a sign of disaster to come.*

Mermaid

Mermaids are creatures of legend. There are many old stories about mermaids. They have long hair and the head and body of a woman. Their lower half is a long, scaly fish tail. They live in the sea.

In stories, mermaids sat on rocks or shores. They often sang sweetly. Sailors passing by in ships heard their lovely songs. They tried to follow the mermaids and wrecked their ships on the rocks.

Metal

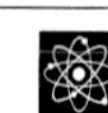

There are more than a hundred ELEMENTS on the Earth. About two-thirds of these are metals. The most important metals are IRON (for making steel), COPPER and ALUMINIUM.

People have used metals since early times. Copper, TIN and IRON were the first metals to be used. They were made into tools and weapons. GOLD and SILVER were also known very early on. They are often made into jewellery.

Most metals are shiny. They all let heat and electricity pass through them. Copper and silver are the best for this. Nearly all metals are solid unless they are heated.

▼ *This map shows known metal deposits throughout the world, but there must be many more deposits waiting to be discovered.*

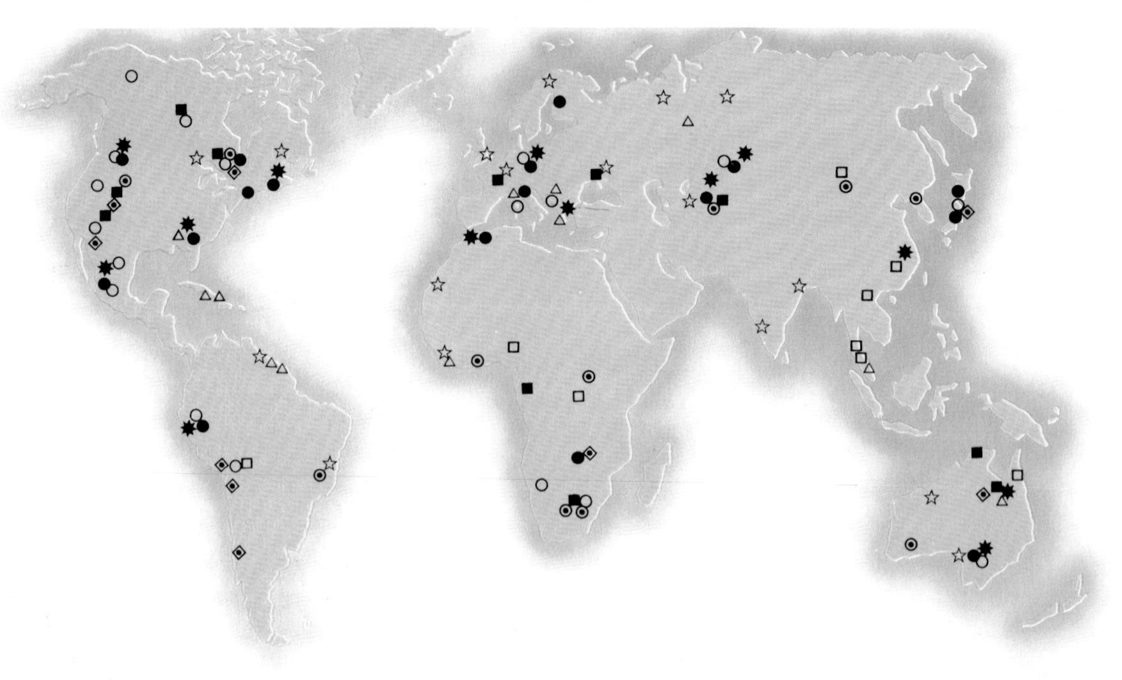

▲ *Metals in the form of ore, such as this lump of iron, are quite unrecognizable except to an expert. The photo of polished titanium (left) was taken through a very powerful microscope.*

Some metals are soft. They are easy to beat into shapes, and they can be pulled into thin wires. Other metals are *brittle*. This means they break easily. Some metals are very hard. It is difficult to work with them.

Metals can be mixed together to form ALLOYS. Alloys are different from their parent metals. Tin and copper are both soft. When mixed together, they form bronze. Bronze is a strong alloy. It is hard enough for swords and spears.

Metals are found in the ground. Some are found pure. They are not mixed with other things. Many metals are mixed up with other elements in MINERALS. The minerals must be treated to get the pure metal out.

Metals vary so much that it is difficult to say exactly what a metal is. The metal lithium is so light it floats easily on water – it is only half the weight of the same volume of water. Osmium is 22 times as heavy as water – twice as heavy as lead. Pure gold is so soft that 20 grams of it can be drawn out into an unbroken wire 50 km long.

Meteor

A meteor is a tiny piece of metal or stone. It travels through space at great speed. Millions of meteors fall on the Earth every day. Most of them burn up before they reach the ground. On clear nights you can sometimes see shooting stars. They are meteors burning up. Sometimes a large meteor reaches the ground. Then it is called a meteorite. Meteorites sometimes make large holes called craters.

▼ *As a meteor enters the Earth's atmosphere, friction heats it and makes it glow.*

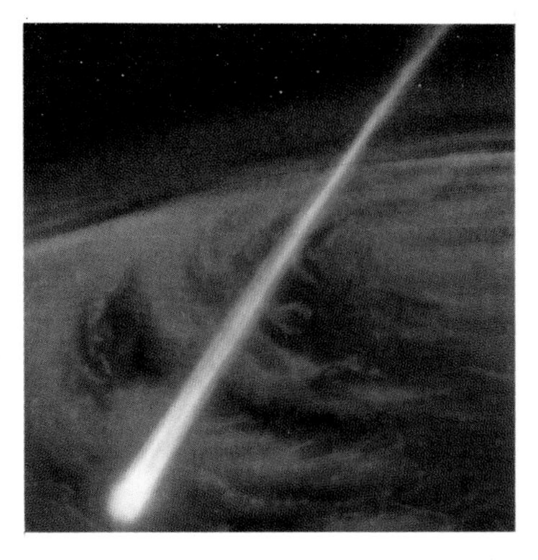

Metric System

The metric system is used for measuring weight, length and volume. It is based on units of ten, or decimals. It was first used in France in the late 1700s. Now it is used in most parts of the world.

MEXICO

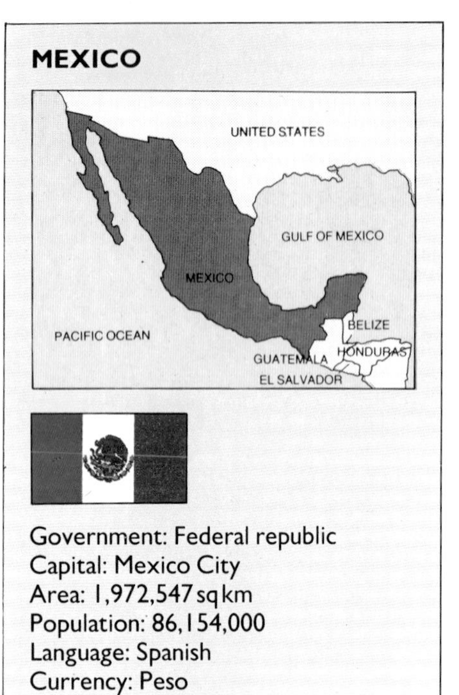

Government: Federal republic
Capital: Mexico City
Area: 1,972,547 sq km
Population: 86,154,000
Language: Spanish
Currency: Peso

Mexico

Mexico is a country in NORTH AMERICA. It lies between the United States in the north and Central America in the south. To the east is the Gulf of Mexico, a big bay. On the west lies the Pacific Ocean.

Mexico has an area of 1,972,547 sq km. Much of the country is hilly, with fertile uplands. The highest mountains reach over 5700 metres. In the south-east, the low Yucatan Peninsula sticks out far into the Gulf of Mexico.

Mexico is a tropical country, but most of the land is high. This makes the climate cool and dry. The north has desert in places.

The first people in Mexico were Indians, such as the AZTECS.

► *Many Mexicans are Roman Catholics and they celebrate their religious festivals with processions and street parties.*

▲ *Michelangelo's statue of David is now housed indoors for protection at the Academy of Fine Arts in Florence.*

Michelangelo

Michelangelo Buonarroti (1475–1564) was a painter and sculptor. He lived in Italy at the time of the RENAISSANCE. Michelangelo is famous for the wonderful statues and paintings he made of people. He spent four and a half years painting pictures in the Sistine Chapel in the VATICAN CITY. Many of his statues are large and very lifelike. His statue of David is 4 metres high. Michelangelo was the chief architect of St Peter's in Rome.

Microphone

A microphone picks up SOUND waves and turns them into electric signals. The signals can be made into a RECORDING or sent out as RADIO waves. They can also be fed through an amplifier and loudspeakers. These make the sound louder. The mouthpiece of a TELEPHONE has a microphone in it that turns your voice into electric signals.

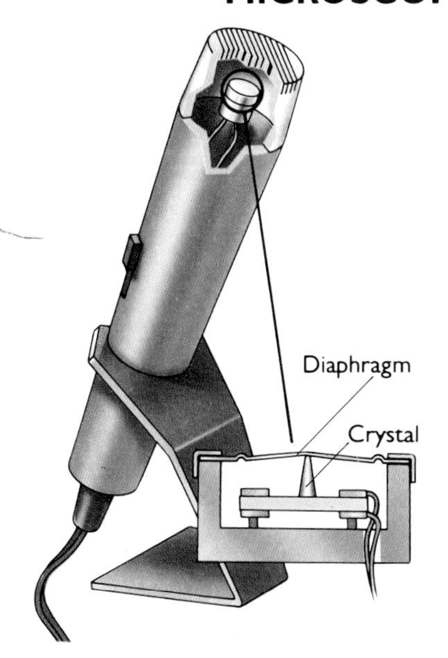

▲ *In this microphone, sound waves hit the flexible diaphragm and make it vibrate. These vibrations are picked up by a crystal and turned into electric signals.*

Microscope

A microscope is an instrument used for looking at tiny objects. It *magnifies* things, or makes them look bigger. Things that are invisible to the naked eye are called *microscopic*. Many microscopic plants and animals, including BACTERIA, can be seen if you look at them through a microscope.

Microscopes work by using lenses. The simplest microscope is a magnifying glass. It has only one LENS. The lenses in many microscopes work by bending light rays. Small microscopes can magnify 100 times. Big microscopes used by scientists may magnify up to 1600 times. The electron microscope is much more powerful. It can magnify up to 2,000,000 times. Instead of bending light rays, it bends beams of electrons. Electrons are parts of ATOMS.

Anton van Leeuwenhoek, a Dutchman who lived

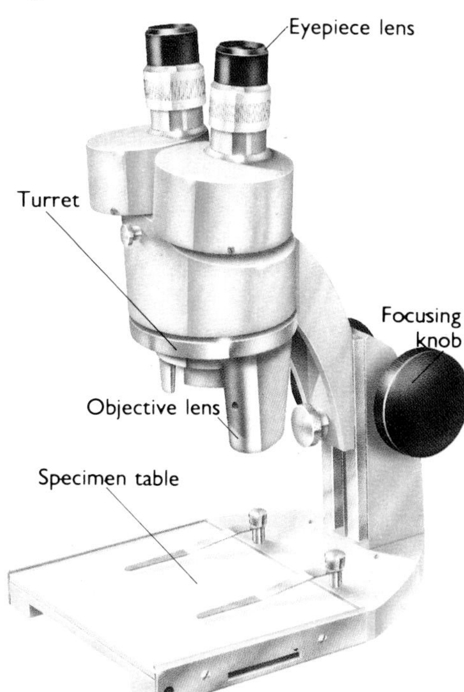

▲ *In an optical microscope, the image can be seen by looking down through the eyepiece and tube, containing a series of magnifying lenses.*

◀ *This electron microscope image shows a dust mite, flakes of skin, soil particles, cat fur and fibres, all taken from a vacuum cleaner.*

in the 1600s, made one of the first microscopes. Using his microscope, he showed that fleas hatch from tiny eggs. Before this, people thought fleas came from sand or mud. They could not see the eggs.

The world's most powerful electron microscopes can magnify objects up to about two million times. Measurements as small as one ten-billionth of a metre can be observed.

Middle Ages

The Middle Ages was a period of history in Europe which lasted for a thousand years. The Middle Ages began when the ROMAN EMPIRE collapsed in the 400s. They ended when the RENAISSANCE began in the 1400s. (See pages 442-443.)

Migration

Many animals make long journeys to breed or find food. Most make the journey every year. Some make the journey only twice in their life. These journeys are called migrations. Animals migrate by INSTINCT. They do not have to plan their journey.

Birds are the greatest migrants. Swallows leave Europe and North America every autumn. They fly south to spend winter in Africa or South America.

▲ *Monarch butterflies migrate from Canada and the USA to Mexico in huge numbers each year.*

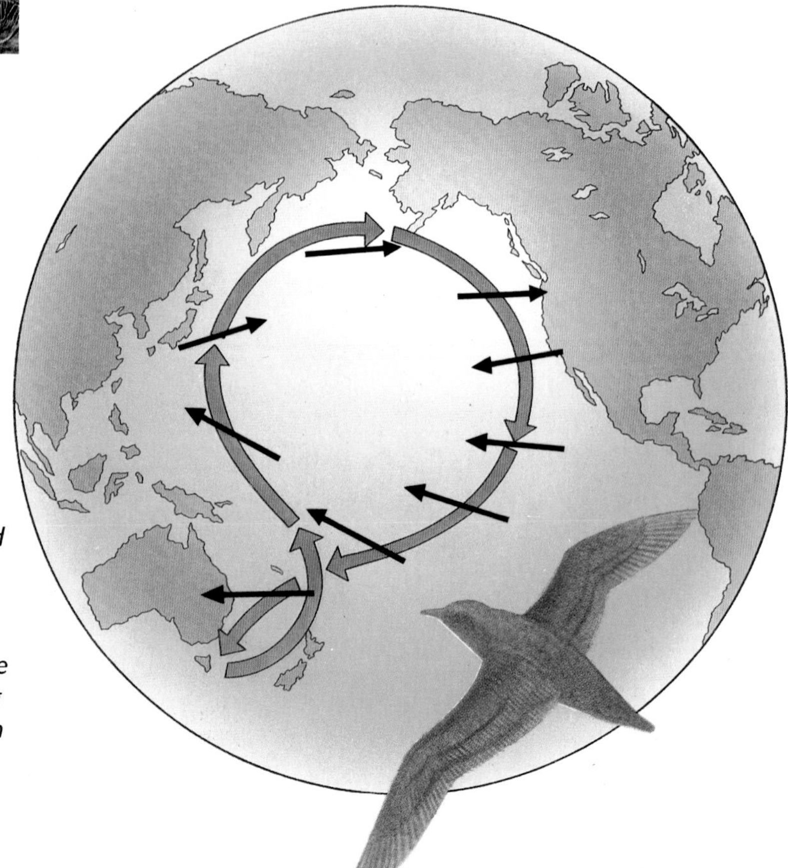

► *Each year, the short-tailed shearwater travels from Tasmania and Australia towards the Pacific. Following the wind, the bird flies all the way to Arctic regions via the Asian coast before returning along the North American coast to its breeding ground. It is a round trip of 32,000 km and takes the bird seven months.*

These places are warm and the swallows find plenty of food there. The trip may be 10,000 km long. In spring, the swallows fly north again to breed.

But birds are not the only animals that make long trips. Butterflies, fish and mammals migrate too. Whales and fish make long journeys through the sea to find food and breed. The EELS of Europe's lakes and rivers swim thousands of kilometres across the Atlantic Ocean to breed. After breeding they die. The young eels take years to swim back to Europe. Monarch butterflies of North America fly south in great numbers for the winter.

The white beluga whale lives in the Arctic and migrates south in the summer and north again in the winter. Scientists are not sure why the whale follows this strange 'upside-down' path of migration.

Milk

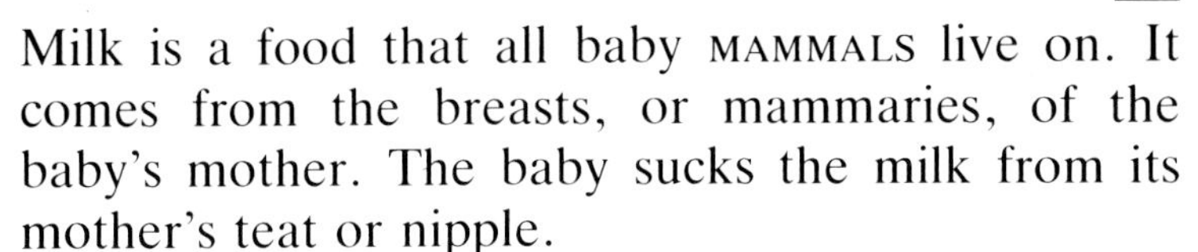

Milk is a food that all baby MAMMALS live on. It comes from the breasts, or mammaries, of the baby's mother. The baby sucks the milk from its mother's teat or nipple.

At first, the milk is pale and watery. It protects the baby from diseases and infections. Later, the milk is much richer and creamier. It contains all the food the baby needs. Milk is full of FAT, SUGAR, STARCHES, PROTEIN, VITAMINS and MINERALS. After a while the baby starts to eat other kinds of food.

People use milk from many animals. These include cows, sheep, goats, camels, and even reindeer. The animals are kept in herds. Sometimes

Continued on page 444

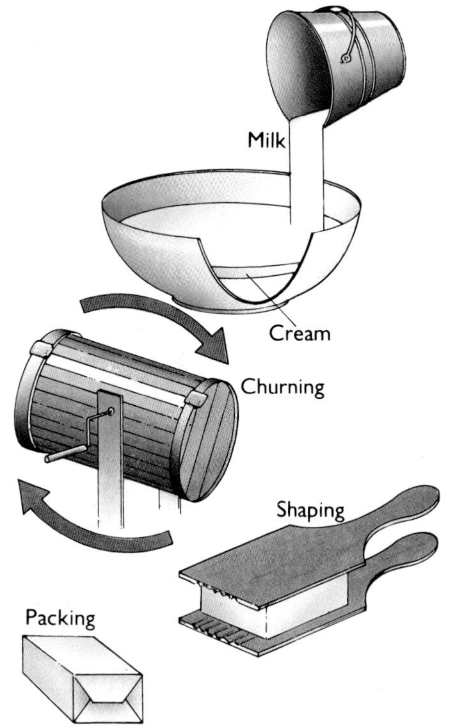

▲ *Traditional methods of making butter involved skimming the cream off milk and 'churning' it by agitating it in a butter churn. This made the fat particles come together to form a thick yellow solid. It was patted into shape with wooden paddles, then wrapped and sold.*

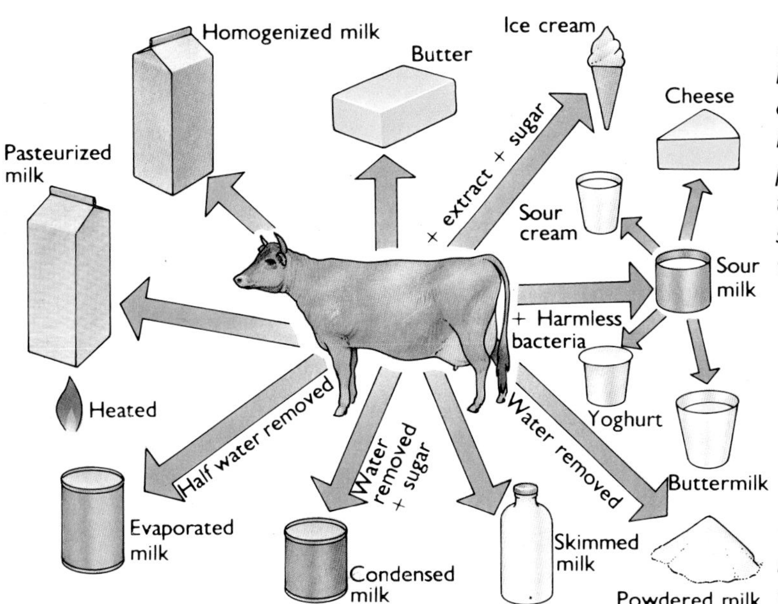

◀ *Many different products can be made from milk by treating it in various ways.*

MIDDLE AGES

The Middle Ages in Europe began with the collapse of the Roman Empire in the AD 400s and lasted for about 1000 years. The 'Roman peace' ended, and much of Europe suffered wars and invasions. The learning of ancient times was almost forgotten, surviving only in the monasteries. Kings and nobles struggled for power, while the mass of the people dwelt in poverty.

However, the Middle Ages also gave much to later generations. Great cathedrals were built. Universities were started. Painting and literature developed. With the 1400s came a rebirth of learning, the Renaissance, and the voyages of discovery to new lands. The Middle Ages were over.

THE CRUSADES

The Crusades were a series of wars between the Christian armies of Europe and the Muslims who had conquered the Holy Land of Palestine. The First Crusade was in 1096, and there were six Crusades in all. The Crusaders captured Jerusalem in 1099, but lost it again in 1187. They were finally defeated by the Muslims in 1303.

Many knights went to the Holy Land, some seeking honour and glory, others riches and lands. Many died before they ever reached Palestine. An important result of these wars was that Europeans learned about Eastern medicine and science, and new trade routes were opened to Asia.

THE MONK

Monks lived in religious communities, or monasteries. They copied out books by hand, and spent much time in prayer. They also tended their farms, gardens and fishponds.

THE KNIGHT

A knight was trained for war. He wore armour and rode a horse. Knights practised fighting at mock-battles called jousts. They were supposed to obey a code of knightly honour, known as chivalry.

THE PEASANT

Peasants worked on the land, and lived in rough huts which they often shared with their animals. They slept on straw mattresses on the floor. They ploughed the fields with ploughs pulled by oxen.

IMPORTANT EVENTS OF THE MIDDLE AGES

476 Fall of Roman Empire
570 Birth of Muhammad, prophet of the Muslim religion, followed by Muslim conquests
732 Charles Martel defeats Muslims and prevents them conquering Europe
800 Charlemagne is crowned first Holy Roman Emperor
896 Alfred, King of England, defeats Danish invaders
988 Christianity reaches Russia
1066 William of Normandy conquers England
1096 First Crusade to the Holy Land
1206 Genghis Khan founds Mongol Empire
1337 Start of Hundred Years' War between France and England
1347–51 Black Death (plague) in Europe

DID YOU KNOW ...?

* In the Middle Ages, Latin was the language used by scholars throughout Europe
* People did not have potatoes or sugar to eat, or tea and coffee to drink
* The Black Death was spread by rats and killed 25 million people throughout Europe

◀ *In the feudal system, society was organized in a sort of pyramid, with the clergy and nobles at the top and a great many peasants at the bottom. In the middle were the scientists, merchants, craftsmen and yeoman farmers.*

THE SCIENTIST

Most medieval scientists practised the mysteries of alchemy (trying to turn lead into gold). A few, such as Roger Bacon (1214–1294), studied the stars and realized that the Earth was round. Bacon also experimented with gunpowder.

THE MERCHANT

Merchants bought and sold goods such as furs and wool. Some became very wealthy and started the first banks. Merchants and craftsmen formed powerful associations called guilds. They sold their goods at fairs, at which people gathered to trade and have fun.

For more information turn to these articles: ALCHEMY; ARMOUR; BACON, ROGER; BLACK DEATH; CASTLE; CATHEDRAL; CHAUCER, GEOFFREY; HUNDRED YEARS' WAR; KNIGHT; MONASTERY.

It is impossible to imagine the size of the Milky Way. It takes light from the Sun eight minutes to reach us (the Sun is 150,000,000 km away and light travels at a speed of 300,000 km per second). Light from the centre of the Milky Way takes about 30,000 *years* to reach the Earth. From where we are in the solar system it takes about 200 million years for the Earth to make just one trip around the Milky Way.

they live on farms. Reindeer do not live on farms but wander about in the wild.

Milk is used to make many other foods. Cream, butter, yoghurt, cheese and some ice cream are all made from milk.

Milky Way

When you look at the sky on a clear, moonless night you can see a pale cloud of light. It stretches across the heavens. If you look at it through binoculars or a telescope, you can see that the cloud is really millions of stars. All these stars, and most of the other stars we see, are part of our GALAXY. It is called the Milky Way.

Astronomers think that the Milky Way has about 100,000 million stars like our Sun. The Milky Way stretches over a distance of about 100,000 light-years. A light-year is the distance light travels in one year at a speed of 300,000 km a second. Our own SOLAR SYSTEM is 30,000 light-years from the centre of the Milky Way.

The Milky Way has a spiral shape. Its trailing arms turn slowly around the centre. They take 200 million years to make a full circle. From Earth, we see the Milky Way through the arms of the spiral. The cloud of stars in the picture is what we might see from a great distance above the galaxy.

▼ *The view below shows how the Milky Way might appear from a few hundred light-years above the galaxy.*

The Milky Way is not a special galaxy. There are thousands of other galaxies with the same shape. There may be millions and millions of other galaxies in the UNIVERSE.

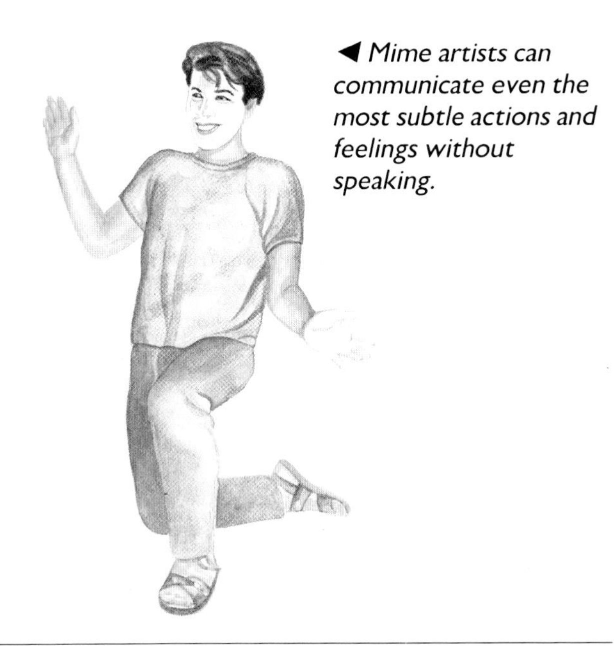

◀ *Mime artists can communicate even the most subtle actions and feelings without speaking.*

Mime

Mime is the art of acting in silence. A mime artist does not speak. Instead, his or her movements tell the story. The face, hands and body are used to show how the artist feels. Mime artists are like dancers. They must control every movement with great care so that the audience can follow the story.

Mime was popular in ancient Greece and Rome. Then it was noisy and included a lot of acrobatics and juggling. The actors wore masks. Mime was also popular in the Middle Ages. Later, entire plays were mimed without words. Mime is used a lot in dancing, especially ballet.

Mineral

The rocks of the Earth are made up of materials called minerals. There are many different kinds of mineral. Some, such as GOLD or platinum, are made up of only one ELEMENT. Others, such as QUARTZ and SALT, consist of two or more elements. Some minerals are metals, such as COPPER or SILVER. Other minerals are non-metallic, like SULPHUR.

▼ *A scale of hardness of minerals was devised by an Austrian, Friedrich Mohs, with the softest at the top and the hardest at the bottom. They are classed from 1 to 10. The hardness of other common things is shown alongside. Each mineral can scratch those above it on the scale, but not below.*

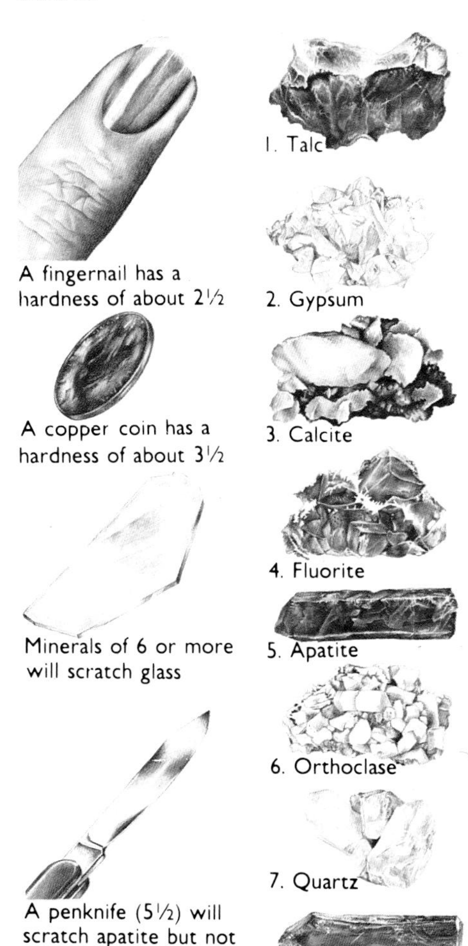

8. Topaz

9. Corundum

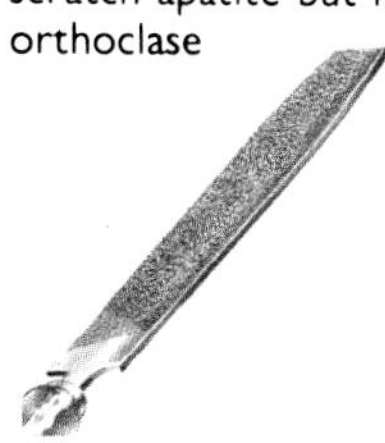

A special steel file will scratch quartz

10. Diamond

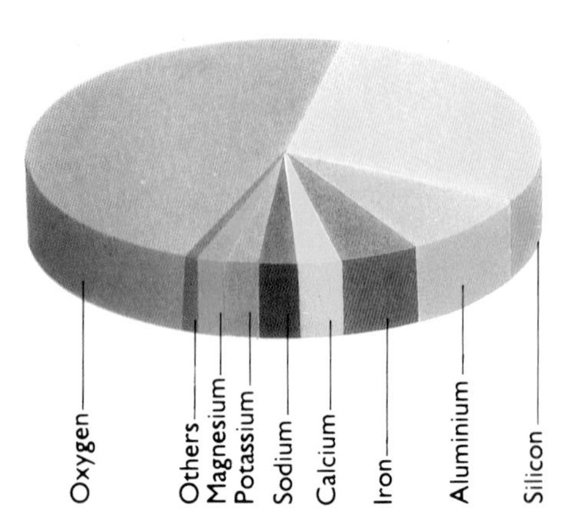

▲ *This chart shows the various elements, including minerals, found in the Earth's crust. They are shown in the proportions in which they occur.*

Pure minerals are made up of ATOMS arranged in regular patterns, known as CRYSTALS. Minerals form crystals when they cool from hot GASES and LIQUIDS deep inside the Earth. Crystals can grow very large if they cool slowly. But large or small, crystals of the same mineral nearly always have the same shape.

Altogether there are over 2000 minerals. Yet most of the Earth's rocks are made up of only 30 minerals. The most common mineral of all is quartz. Most grains of sand are quartz. Pure quartz is made up of large, well-shaped crystals and has a milky colour.

Mining

Mining means digging MINERALS out of the Earth. It is one of the world's most important industries. When minerals lie in one place in large quantities they are known as ores. People mine minerals such as GOLD, SILVER and TIN. They also mine COAL.

Mines can be open pits or underground tunnels. When the ore is close to the surface the soil that lies on top of it is simply lifted away. Giant diggers then scoop up the rock that contains the minerals. Underground mines can be as deep as 3 km below the surface. Another form of mining is dredging. Here minerals are scooped up from the beds of rivers and lakes.

The 'Big Hole', at Kimberley, South Africa, is an old disused diamond mine that was dug out last century by thousands of miners working with picks and shovels. They dug out more than 25 million tonnes of rock to make a hole 500 m across and nearly 400 m deep.

► *The Kennecott open-pit copper mine in Utah is the largest in the USA.*

◀ *This solar furnace in France uses a huge curved mirror to focus the Sun's rays and produce temperatures as high as 3000°C.*

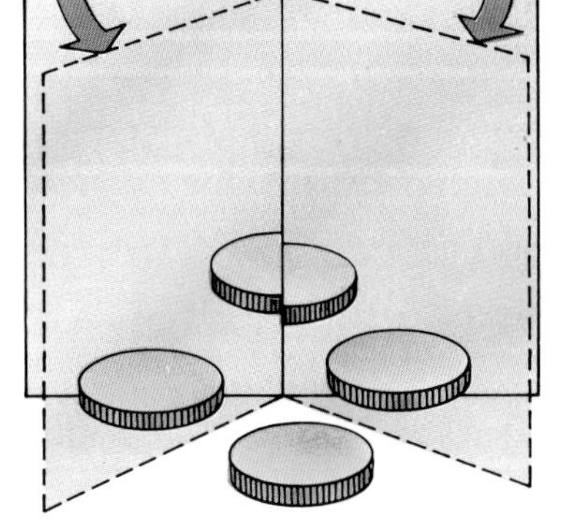

SEE IT YOURSELF

It is possible to see a reflection of a reflection. Lay a coin on a table. Take two mirrors and hold them next to each other with the edges touching as shown above. Now move the outer edges of the mirrors slowly forward, while keeping the inner edges together. How many coins can you see?

Mirror

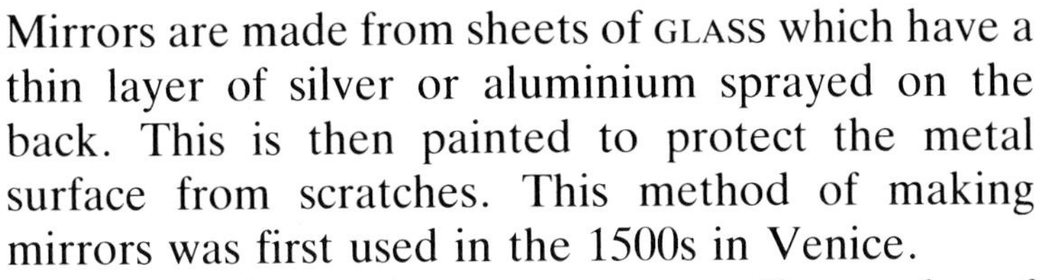

Mirrors are made from sheets of GLASS which have a thin layer of silver or aluminium sprayed on the back. This is then painted to protect the metal surface from scratches. This method of making mirrors was first used in the 1500s in Venice.

Before then mirrors were usually made of polished metal such as silver or bronze. Some mirrors from ancient Egypt are almost 5000 years old. LIGHT is reflected from (bounces off) a smooth surface. The reflection, called an image, is what we see when we look into a mirror, but the image is reversed. If you raise your left hand, the image raises its right hand.

A plane mirror has a flat surface. A convex mirror curves outwards like the back of a spoon. A concave mirror curves inwards like a hollow bowl.

Mississippi River

The Mississippi River is the longest river in the UNITED STATES. It rises in Minnesota in the north and flows 3780 km southwards to the Gulf of Mexico. It has over 250 tributaries, small rivers that flow into it. The waters of the Mississippi

Probably the earliest model was found in an ancient Egyptian tomb. It is a model boat and is about 4000 years old. The Egyptians believed that the dead person's spirit needed help to cross the River of the Dead, so they buried model ships in the tomb. In the Middle Ages, sailors often carved model ships and hung them in churches as thanksgiving offerings for being saved from storms at sea.

carry a lot of mud. As a result its DELTA, where most of the mud is dumped, is growing out to sea at a rate of a kilometre every 10 years.

Models

Models may be small copies of larger objects. Model planes, cars and trains are all examples of this type of model. Another kind of model is of something that does not yet exist, such as an architect's model of a new building or a design for a new aircraft. Models are used to test products, in teaching, and for special effects in film-making. Materials for models include balsa wood, card and glue, though today there are many kits available for making all kinds of models at home.

Mole

Moles are small burrowing animals. They are found all over the world. They have narrow snouts and large clawed feet for tunnelling quickly through the soil.

Moles spend most of their lives underground. Their eyes are almost useless but they have good hearing and very sensitive noses for finding food. Moles feed mainly on worms and grubs.

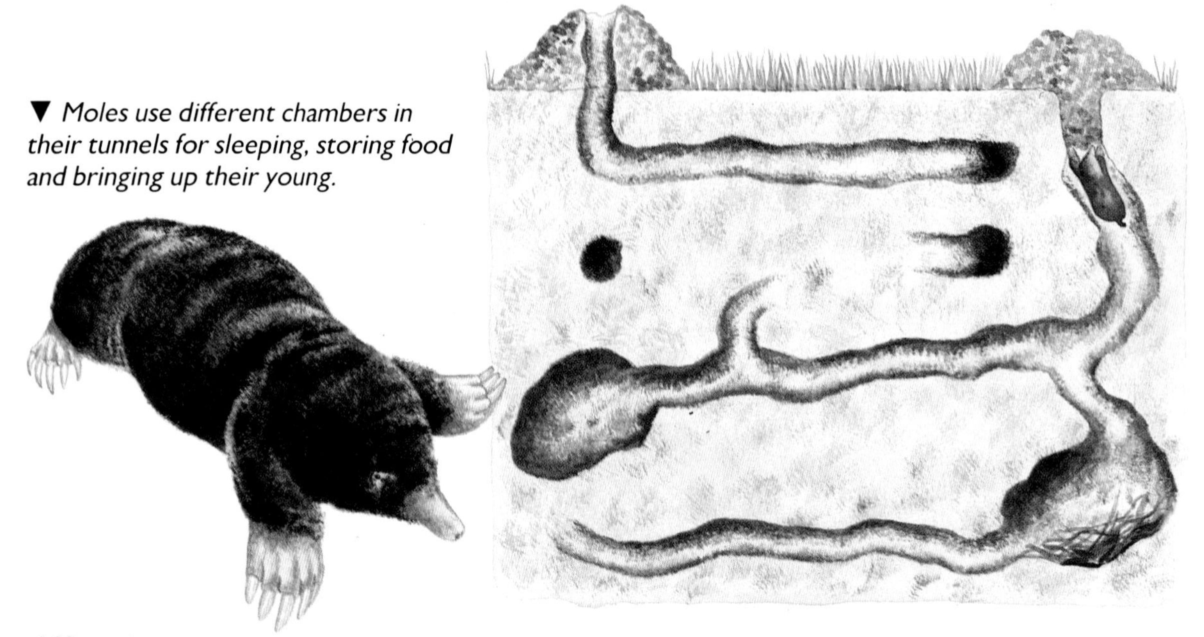

▼ *Moles use different chambers in their tunnels for sleeping, storing food and bringing up their young.*

▲ *A great variety of molluscs are found in the sea, and some of them are good to eat.*

Mollusc

Molluscs are a large group of animals. There are about 70,000 different kinds. After insects they are the most numerous of all animals. They are found everywhere from deserts and mountains to the depths of the sea.

Most molluscs grow shells to protect themselves; some have shells inside parts of their bodies; some have no shells at all. But all molluscs have soft bodies and no bones. And all molluscs have to stay moist to live.

Some shells are only a few millimetres wide. Others, such as that of the giant clam, are over a metre wide. As a mollusc grows, its shell grows with it. The shell is made of a hard limy material formed from the food the mollusc eats. Shells have many strange shapes and patterns and some of them are very beautiful.

The largest mollusc is the giant squid. This can grow to as much as 12 metres.

Monaco

The tiny country of Monaco lies on the French coast of the Mediterranean Sea. It has an area of less than two square km. It is called a principality because it is ruled by a prince. Monaco's main industry is tour-

MONACO

SWITZERLAND
FRANCE
ITALY
MONACO
MEDITERRANEAN SEA

Government: Constitutional monarchy
Capital: Monaco-Ville
Area: 1.9 sq km
Population: 29,000
Language: French
Currency: French franc

With a population of 28,000 in an area of 1.9 square kilometres, Monaco has a greater population density than any other country in the world – 14,000 people per square kilometre. The United Kingdom's density is 377 per square kilometre.

ism. More than half of the people of Monaco are French.

Monaco has been ruled by the Grimaldi family since the 1200s.

Monastery

Monasteries are places where monks live in a community, or group. They lead a religious life and obey strict rules. Monasteries are especially important in the BUDDHIST and CHRISTIAN religions.

Christian monasteries began in Egypt around AD 300. Hermits were religious men who lived alone. A group of hermits came together and made rules for their way of life. Soon after, communities of monks began to grow up. The monks worked as farmers, labourers and teachers, and helped the poor.

One of the most famous monks was St Benedict. He founded the Benedictine order. Many groups of monks followed his rules for running a monastery. St Benedict divided the day into periods of prayer, religious study and work.

The world's most famous monastery is that at Monte Cassino in central Italy. It was founded in AD 529 by St Benedict, and it was there that he gathered round him the first group of Benedictine monks. The monastery has led a troubled life. It was stormed by the Lombards in 589, the Saracens in 884 and by the Normans in 1030. Each time it was refounded on the same site and became a great centre of the arts and learning. During World War II it was the scene of heavy fighting as the German army retreated before the Allied advance. Then, on February 15, 1944, the monastery was almost completely demolished by Allied bombers. Most of its valuable art collection was destroyed but many treasured manuscripts were saved. The monastery has been rebuilt.

▶ *In monasteries, a great deal of time is devoted to prayer, with regular services and ceremonies every day.*

THE DEVELOPMENT OF MONEY

The earliest form of trade was bartering, when goods would simply be exchanged.

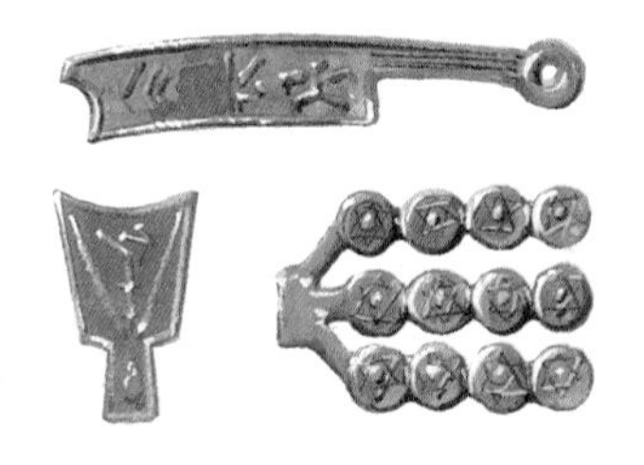

Money has been made in all shapes and sizes, but it must be easy to use and store.

American Indians used beads and shells, often made into decorative patterns, as money.

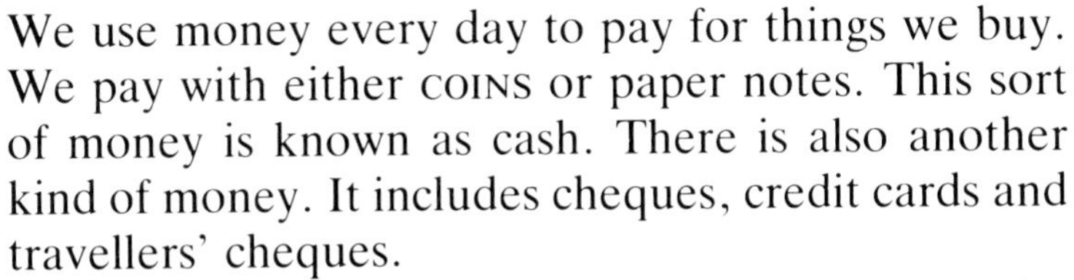

Money

We use money every day to pay for things we buy. We pay with either COINS or paper notes. This sort of money is known as cash. There is also another kind of money. It includes cheques, credit cards and travellers' cheques.

Almost anything can be used as money. In the past people have used shells, beads, cocoa beans, salt, grain and even cattle. But coins are much easier to use than say, cattle. They are easy to store and to carry around.

Coins were first used in China. They were also used by ancient Greeks as early as 600 BC. They were valuable because they were made of either gold or silver. They were stamped with the mark of the government or the ruler of the country for which they were made. The stamp also showed how much each coin was worth.

Later, people began to use coins made of cheaper metals. The metal itself had no value, but the coins were still worth the amount stamped on them. They also started to use paper money. It no longer mattered that the money itself had no real value. It was backed by the government and BANKS. This is the kind of money we use today.

Coins have remained popular for centuries. They are easy to produce and last a long time.

Bank notes are a kind of promise, because they represent a sum of money.

Credit cards and cheques are useful because they can be used instead of cash.

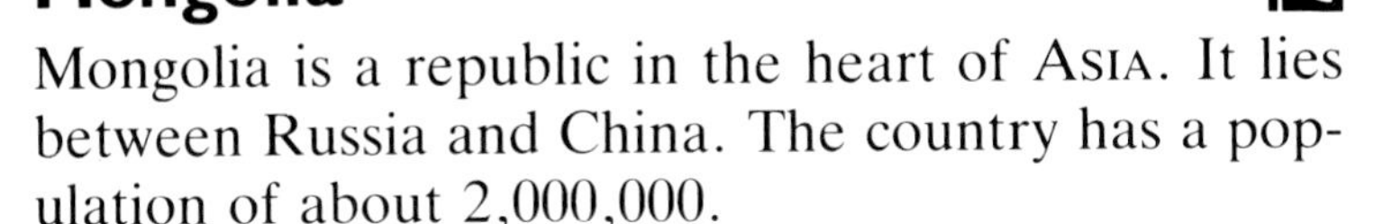

Mongolia

Mongolia is a republic in the heart of ASIA. It lies between Russia and China. The country has a population of about 2,000,000.

MONGOLIA

Government: Multi-party system
Capital: Ulan Bator
Area: 1,565,000 sq km
Population: 2,100,000
Language: Mongolian
Currency: Tugrik

Mongolia is a high, flat country. It is mostly desert or rolling grassland, with mountain ranges in the west. The Gobi Desert covers a large part of the land.

The people of Mongolia are descended from the MONGOLS. Until recently a Communist state, Mongolia now has a multi-party system.

Mongols

Mongols were NOMADS who lived on the great plains of central Asia. They herded huge flocks of sheep, goats, cattle and horses, which they grazed on the vast grasslands of the region. They lived in tent villages that they could quickly pack up and take with them when they moved on to find new pastures.

The Mongols were superb horsemen and highly trained warriors. In the 1200s they formed a mighty army under the great GENGHIS KHAN. Swift-riding hordes of Mongols swept through China, India, Persia and as far west as Hungary.

Under Genghis Khan, and later his grandson, Kublai Khan, the Mongols conquered half the known world. But they were unable to hold their empire together. In less than 100 years the Mongol empire had been taken over by the Chinese.

▼ *Mongols were wanderers and expert horsemen. Their temporary shelters, known as yurts, were made of wood and hides.*

◀ *In a story by Rudyard Kipling, a mongoose called Rikki-Tikki-Tavi bravely kills a snake.*

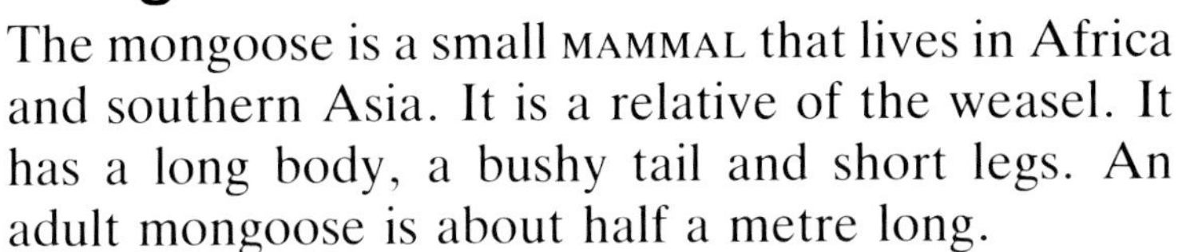

Mongoose

The mongoose is a small MAMMAL that lives in Africa and southern Asia. It is a relative of the weasel. It has a long body, a bushy tail and short legs. An adult mongoose is about half a metre long.

Mongooses live in burrows and feed on small birds, poultry, mice and rats. Their fierceness and speed also helps them to kill dangerous snakes like the cobra.

Monkey

Monkeys are MAMMALS that belong to the same group of animals as APES and HUMAN BEINGS. Most monkeys have long tails and thick fur all over their body. Monkeys are usually smaller than apes. Their hands and feet are used for grasping and are very similar to those of humans.

There are about 400 different kinds of monkey. Most live in the tropics, especially in forests, in Africa, Asia and South America. South American monkeys have long tails that they use like an extra arm or leg when swinging through the branches of trees.

On the ground monkeys usually move about on all four limbs. But when they are using their hands to hold something they can stand or sit up on two legs.

Monkeys live in family groups known as troops. They spend a lot of time chattering, playing, fighting and grooming each other. Each troop of monkeys has its own territory where it lives and feeds. It will fight fiercely to defend this area against other invading groups.

▲ *The colobus and mandrill are both Old World monkeys living in Africa. The colobus has no thumb and the mandrill is one of the largest monkeys. New World monkeys, including the spider and woolly monkeys, live in the forests of South America. They have long* prehensile *tails that can be used as an extra 'hand'.*

Monsoon

Monsoons are winds that blow from land to sea during winter, and from sea to land during summer. They occur mainly in southern Asia. The summer monsoon carries moisture from the sea, and rain falls over the land. Summer monsoons bring the rainy season. In India, about 1700mm of rain fall between June and September, and only another 100mm in all the rest of the year.

Since ancient times, sailors have used the seasonal turn around of the monsoon winds on their voyages. Sailing ships in the Arabian Sea sail westwards from India to Africa when the monsoon blows towards the south-west. In summer, the monsoon blows from the south-west and the trading vessels return to India.

Moon

The Moon is our nearest neighbour in space. It loops around the EARTH, never coming closer than 361,000km. It travels at about 3660km/hr and takes 27¹/₃ days to complete the circuit. (See pages 456–457.)

Moore, Henry

Henry Moore (1898–1986) was a famous British sculptor who worked in wood, stone and metal. His carvings are usually large and are easily recognized by their round, curving shapes and smooth lines.

Moore is also well known for his drawings. His pictures of people sheltering underground during the air raids of World War II are especially famous.

▲ *This bronze sculpture by Henry Moore is typical of his simple, uncluttered style of work.*

Mormon

Mormons belong to a religious group founded by Joseph Smith in 1830. The name comes from the *Book of Mormon*, which Mormons believe is a sacred history of ancient American peoples. The Mormons began in New York, but were persecuted for their beliefs and driven out. They finally settled in Salt Lake Valley, Utah.

Morocco

Morocco is a country right at the top of north-west AFRICA. It is nearly twice the size of Great Britain and has two coastlines. On the west is the Atlantic Ocean and to the north is the Mediterranean Sea.

MOROCCO

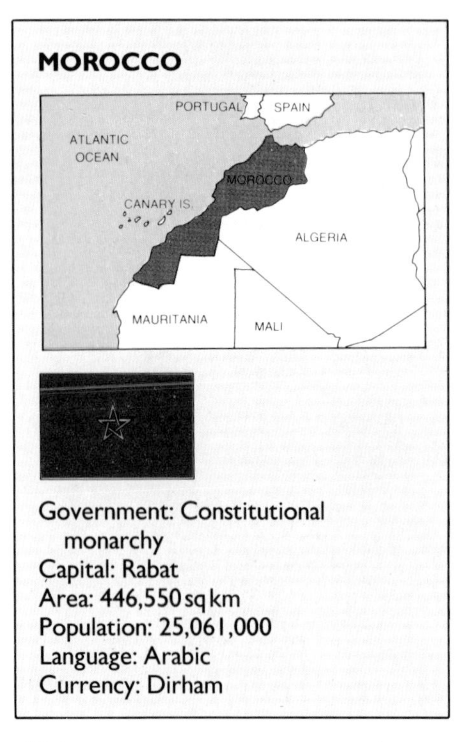

Government: Constitutional monarchy
Capital: Rabat
Area: 446,550sq km
Population: 25,061,000
Language: Arabic
Currency: Dirham

Most of Morocco's 25 million people are farmers. They grow wheat, maize, fruit, olives and nuts. Some keep sheep, goats and cattle. Most of the people are Muslims. Casablanca is the largest city and main seaport. The country is ruled by a king.

Morse Code

Morse code is a simple way of sending messages. It is an alphabet of dots and dashes. Each letter has its own dot and dash pattern. The code was invented by Samuel Morse, an American artist, to send messages along a telegraph wire. The telegraph operator presses a key at one end to send a signal along the wire to a sounder at the other end. A short signal is a dot and a long signal is a dash. The first official telegraph message was sent in 1844.

INTERNATIONAL MORSE CODE

A	·—	P	·——·
B	—···	Q	——·—
C	—·—·	R	·—·
D	—··	S	···
E	·	T	—
F	··—·	U	··—
G	——·	V	···—
H	····	W	·——
I	··	X	—··—
J	·———	Y	—·——
K	—·—	Z	——··
L	·—··	Full stop (.)	·—·—·—
M	——	Comma (,)	——··——
N	—·	Query (?)	··——··
O	———	Error	········

Mosaic

A mosaic is a picture made from small pieces of coloured stone or glass set into cement. The pieces are arranged to make a design or a portrait or to show a scene.

Mosaic making is a very ancient art. The Sumerians made mosaics nearly 5000 years ago. Mosaics are a very practical way of decorating floors and walls, as they can be washed without being spoiled. In ancient Rome, every villa and palace had its

Continued on page 458

The world's largest mosaic adorns four walls in the National University, Mexico City. It shows historical scenes. The two largest mosaic-covered walls are each 1200 square metres in area.

◀ *Roman mosaics like this one in St Albans have been found in many parts of Britain.*

MOON

People have worshipped the Moon, made wishes on the Moon (because of superstition) and even walked on the Moon. The Moon is our nearest neighbour in space. It is the Earth's only natural satellite, and was probably formed at the same time as our planet. But the rocks on the Moon's surface are older than those on the Earth's surface because the Moon has not changed in over 4000 million years.

The Moon is a dry, lifeless world, without air. Gravity on the Moon is just one-sixth of gravity on Earth, yet the Moon's gravitational pull affects us every day. It is the Moon's pull that causes the rise and fall of the ocean tides. Astronauts landed to explore the Moon in 1969. One day in the future permanent bases may be built there.

◀ The Moon has no wind; in fact, no erosion of any kind. This footprint in the Moon-dust, left by an Apollo astronaut, will remain undisturbed for ever.

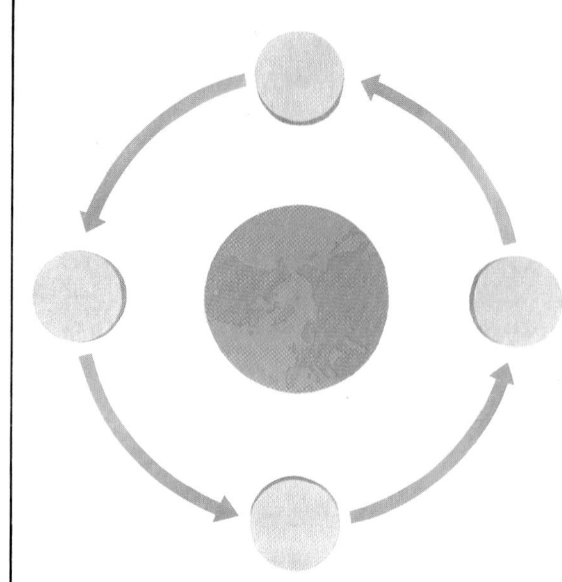

THE MOON'S FACE

When the Moon was newly-formed it was made of molten rock, spinning around once in a few hours. As it cooled, a hard skin or crust formed on the outside. The Earth's gravity, pulling at this crust, slowed the spin down and raised a 'bulge' a few kilometres high on one side. Now this bulge is always turned inwards, and the Moon keeps the same face towards the Earth.

THE PHASES OF THE MOON

The Moon takes just over 27 days to travel around the Earth. It also spins on its own axis, and it always presents the same face to us. The Moon has no light of its own; we see it because it reflects light from the Sun.

When the Moon is between the Earth and the Sun we cannot see it, because the dark side is facing us. Gradually a thin crescent Moon appears – the New Moon. The New Moon waxes (gets larger) and at Full Moon (halfway through its cycle) we see the whole face lit by sunlight. Then the Moon wanes (gets smaller). The interval between one New Moon and the next is 29½ days (longer than the time the Moon takes to orbit the Earth). This is because the Earth itself is moving in space, as it travels around the Sun.

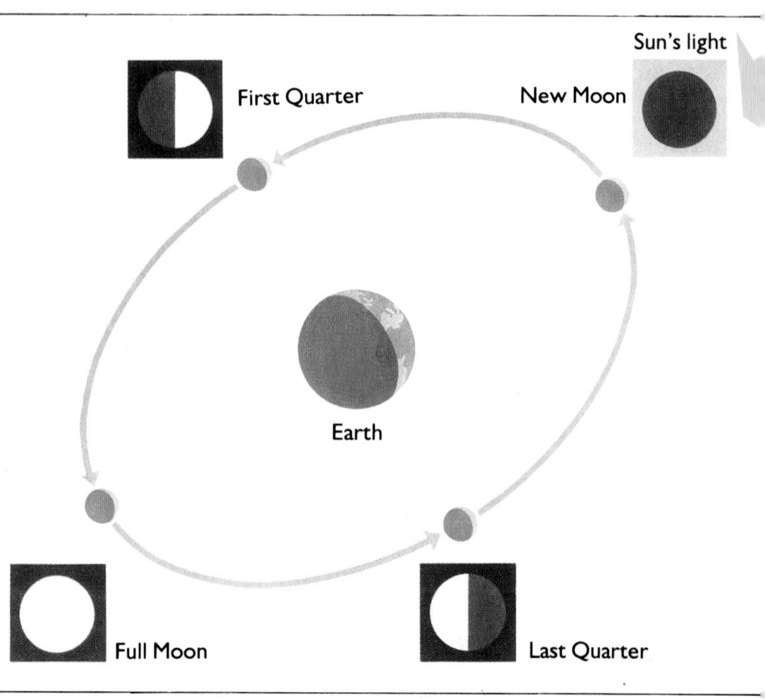

EXPLORING THE MOON

09 Galileo studies the Moon through the newly invented telescope.

47 Johannes Hevelius maps the Moon.

60s First photographs of the Moon.

59 Russian Luna 2 crash-lands on lunar surface. Luna 3 flies around far side.

66 US Orbiter craft photograph Moon in detail to find best landing sites.

68 US Apollo 8 astronauts fly around the Moon.

69 Apollo 11 astronauts land on Moon.

72 Last Apollo Moon-landing.

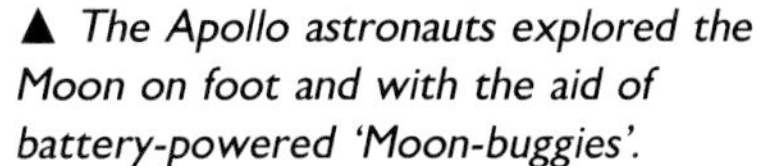

▲ *The Apollo astronauts explored the Moon on foot and with the aid of battery-powered 'Moon-buggies'.*

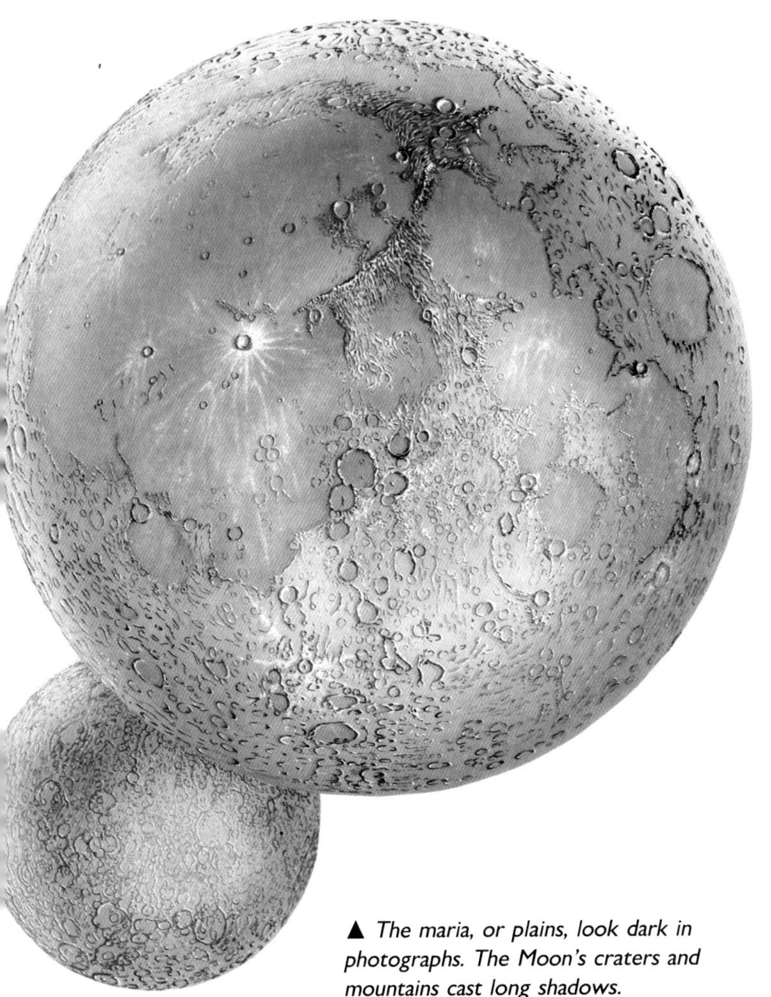

▲ *The maria, or plains, look dark in photographs. The Moon's craters and mountains cast long shadows.*

MOON FACTS

- The Moon is 382,000 kilometres from the Earth.
- The Earth weighs 81 times as much as the Moon.
- The diameter (distance across) of the Moon is 3476 kilometres.
- The oldest Moon rock is 4600 million years old.
- The Moon has no seas. Its flat plains are called maria, because early astronomers mistook them for oceans and named them after the Latin *mare*, meaning 'sea'.
- The Moon's surface is pitted with craters. Almost all these holes were made by meteorites crashing into the Moon.
- The Latin word for the Moon is *luna*. From this we get our word 'lunar', meaning 'of the Moon'.
- The Moon once had active volcanoes, but almost all of its volcanoes are now dead.
- No one on Earth had seen the far side of the Moon until a spacecraft photographed it in 1959.

or more information turn to these articles: ECLIPSE; GALILEO; ORBIT; SATELLITE; SPACE EXPLORATION **and** TIDES.

SEE IT YOURSELF

You can make your own mosaic by using small pebbles, shells, bits of broken china or broken tiles. You will need a board or a very stiff piece of cardboard and some strong glue. Draw your design on the board and decide which colours you will use for each area of the design. Glue the pieces along the edge first and work towards the centre. Glue the pieces as close together as possible. You can put some grout or filler in the spaces between the pieces. This will help to hold your mosaic together.

dazzling mosaics showing scenes from everyday life.

Mosaics were also used to make pictures of saints, angels and JESUS in churches all over Greece, Italy and Turkey.

▲ *St Basil's Cathedral is in one of the most historic parts of Moscow, near Red Square and the Kremlin.*

Moscow

Moscow is the capital of Russia. It is also the biggest city in the country. More than eight million people live there. Moscow lies on a plain across the river Moskva. It is the largest industrial and business centre in the country. Everything is made in Moscow, from cars to clothes. It is also the political and cultural centre of the country.

Moscow was first made the capital of Muscovy in 1547, during the reign of IVAN the Terrible, the first *tsar* (emperor) of Russia. It grew up around the KREMLIN, an ancient fort from which the Muscovy princes used to defend their country. Moscow remained the capital of the tsars until 1712 when Peter the Great moved the capital to St Petersburg. The city remained very important, even after it was nearly all burnt down during NAPOLEON's occupation of 1812. After the Revolution of 1917, Moscow became the seat of the Soviet government. In 1992 it became the capital of Russia again.

Some scholars believe that malaria carried by the mosquito sapped the strength of the people and led to the downfall of the Greek and Roman civilizations.

Mosquito

Mosquitoes are a small kind of FLY. They have slender, tube-shaped bodies, three pairs of long legs and two narrow wings. There are about 1400

different kinds. They live all over the world from the tropics to the Arctic, but must be able to get to water to lay their eggs.

Only female mosquitoes bite and suck blood. They have special piercing mouths. Males live on the juices of plants. When the female bites, she injects a substance into her victim to make the blood flow more easily. This makes mosquito bites itch.

Some kinds of mosquito spread serious diseases. Malaria and yellow fever are two diseases passed on by mosquitoes.

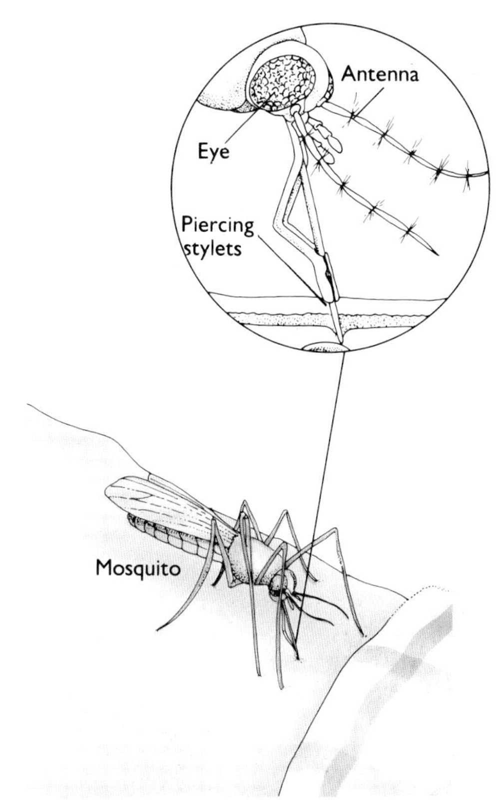

▲ *The female mosquito uses its stylets to pierce tiny blood vessels in its victims.*

Moss

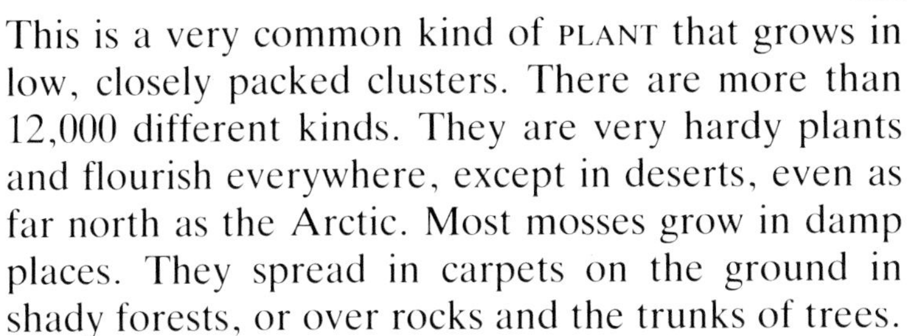

This is a very common kind of PLANT that grows in low, closely packed clusters. There are more than 12,000 different kinds. They are very hardy plants and flourish everywhere, except in deserts, even as far north as the Arctic. Most mosses grow in damp places. They spread in carpets on the ground in shady forests, or over rocks and the trunks of trees.

Mosses are very simple kinds of plants, like LICHENS. They were among the first plants to make their home on land. They have slender creeping stems that are covered with tiny leaves. Instead of proper roots that reach down into the soil, mosses simply have a mass of tiny hairs that soak up moisture and food. Mosses do not have flowers. They reproduce by spores, just like FERNS. One kind, called sphagnum moss, grows in bogs and is the plant that makes peat.

▼ *When mosses are ready to reproduce they produce capsules containing tiny spores. They soak up moisture and nutrients through tiny root-hairs called rhizoids.*

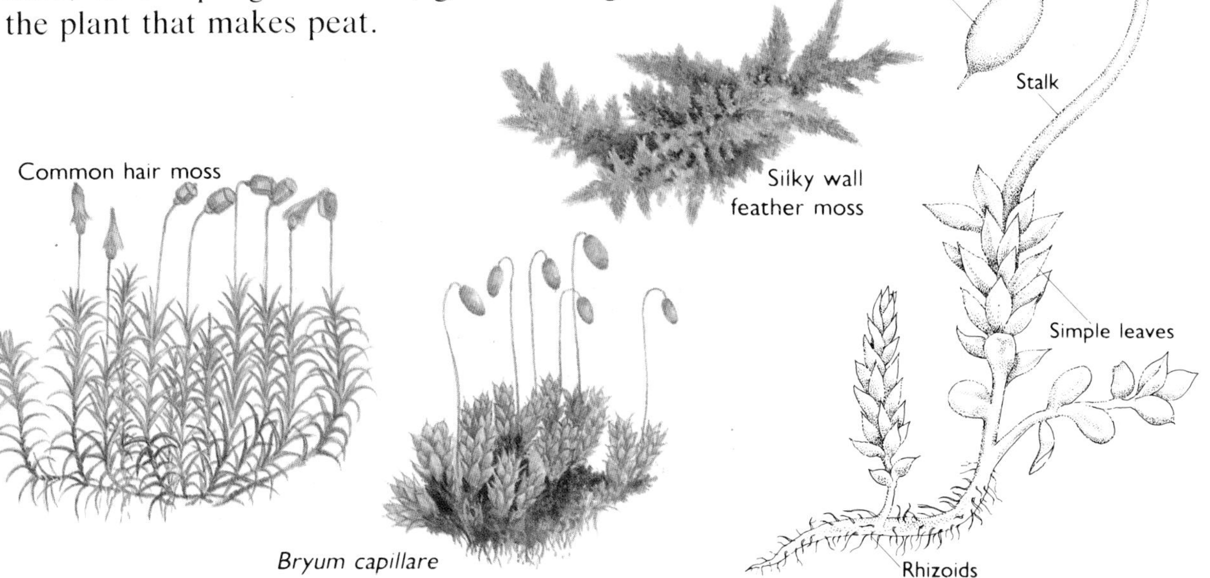

Clothes moths do not really eat clothes. But they lay an enormous number of eggs from which larvae hatch. It is these that devour our clothes and carpets.

Moth

It can be hard to tell moths and BUTTERFLIES apart. These are the signs to look out for. Moths usually fly in the evening and at night, while butterflies can be seen in the daytime. Moths have plumper bodies than butterflies. Moths' antennae are like tiny combs, or have feathery hairs on them. Butterfly antennae end in tiny knobs. When butterflies rest on a plant, they hold their wings upright. Moths spread their wings out flat.

Moths belong to one of the biggest insect groups. There are over 100,000 kinds of moth and they are found all over the world. The smallest scarcely measure 3 mm across. The largest may be bigger than a person's hand. Some moths have very striking colours that warn their enemies that they are poisonous or bad tasting. Moths have a very good sense of smell. They find their food by 'sniffing' their way from plant to plant. A male moth can follow the scent of a female 3 km away.

Moths hatch from eggs, usually in the spring. They hatch into CATERPILLARS. The caterpillar feeds on leaves until it is fully grown. Then it spins itself a silk cocoon. This protects the caterpillar while its body changes into a moth. A few kinds of moth do not spin cocoons, but bury themselves in the ground or in piles of leaves until they grow into moths.

▼ *There is great variety in the appearance of moths and their caterpillars.*

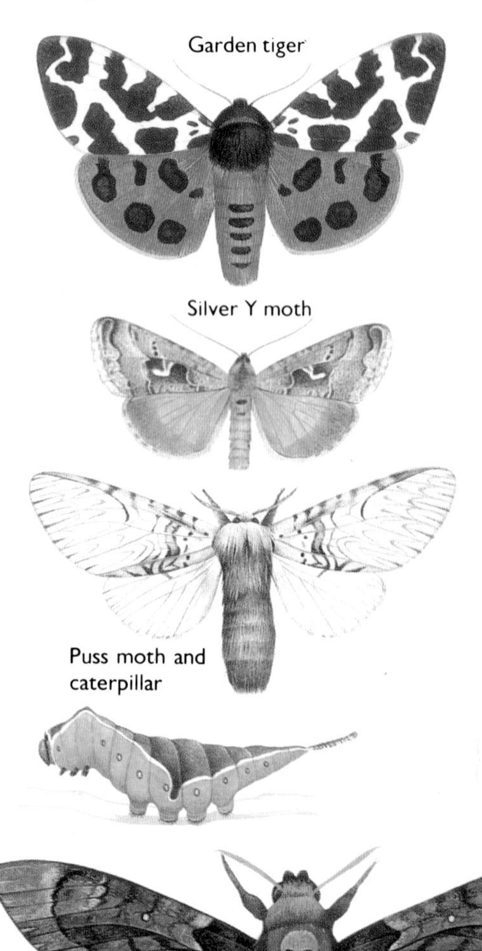

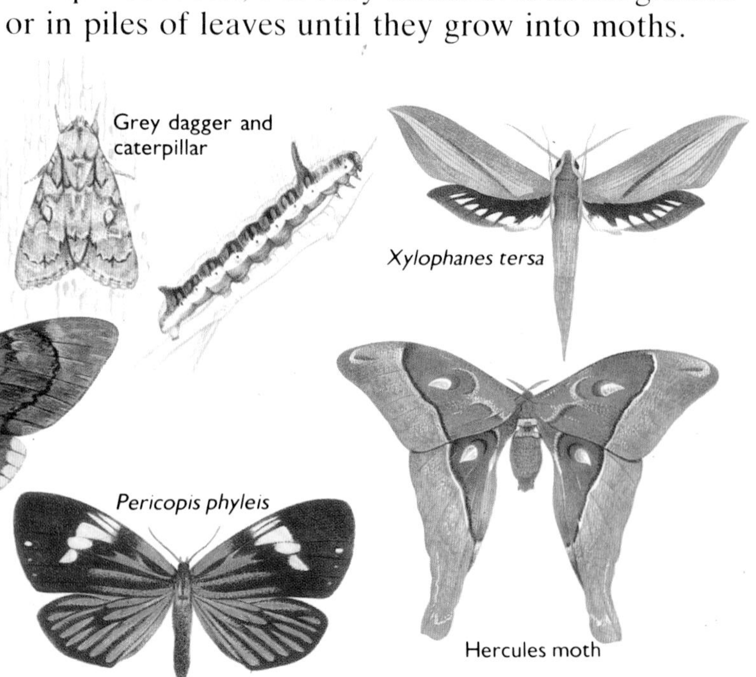

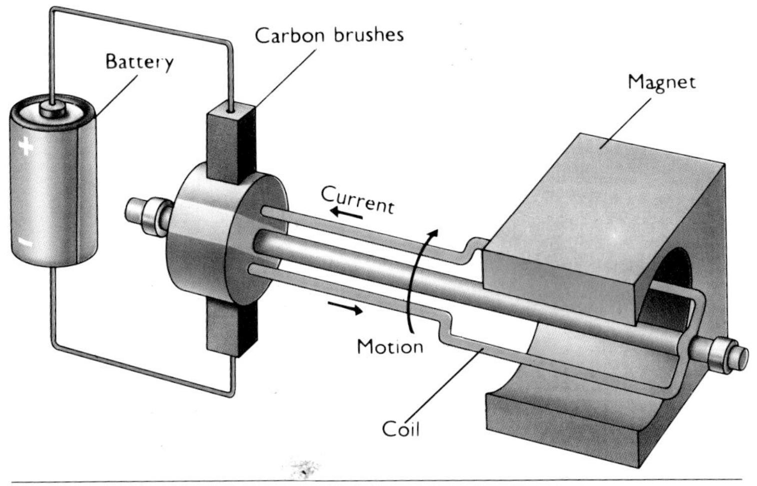

◀ *Simple motors change electric current into mechanical energy. A coil is held between the poles of a permanent magnet. When current flows from the battery, it turns the coil into an electromagnet. The poles of the permanent magnet repel and attract those of the electromagnet, making it spin around. Motors such as these are clean and do not produce fumes.*

Motor, Electric

There are electric motors all around us. Refrigerators, washing machines, electric clocks, vacuum cleaners, hair-dryers and electric mixers are all driven by electric motors. So are some trains and ships.

Electric motors work because the like poles of a magnet repel (push each other apart), and unlike poles attract each other. A simple motor is made up of a coil of wire held between the poles of a magnet. When an electric current flows through the coil, the coil becomes a magnet with a north pole and a south pole. Since like poles repel and unlike poles attract, the coil swings round between the poles of the magnet until its north pole is facing the south pole of the magnet and its south pole is facing the magnet's north pole. The direction of the current in the coil is then reversed so that the coil's poles are also reversed. The coil then has to swing round again to line up its poles with those of the magnet. So the electric motor keeps on turning because it keeps getting a series of magnetic pushes.

▼ *Many household appliances are run by electric motors.*

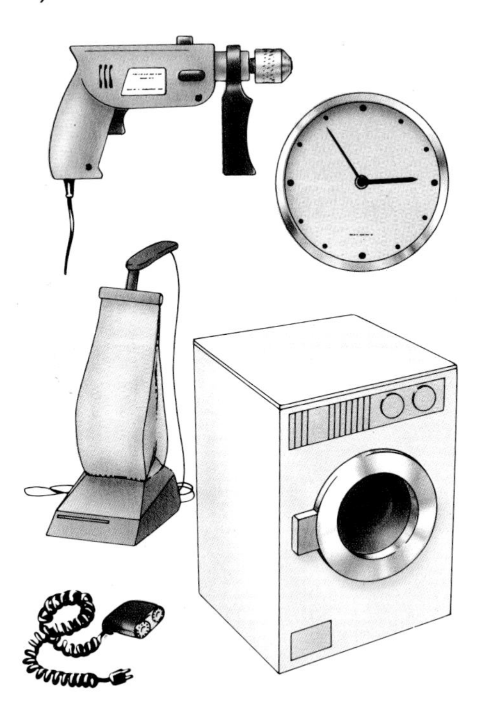

Motor Car

In about a hundred years the motor car has changed the world. The car itself has changed too. The clumsy 'horseless carriage' has become the fast, comfortable and reliable car of today.

Most cars have petrol engines. If petrol is mixed with air and a spark takes place in the mixture, it explodes. The power from this explosion, repeated

The world speed record is held by Richard Noble of Britain. On October 4, 1983 he drove his jet-engined *Thrust 2* at 1019.4 km/h (633.4 mph) on Black Rock Desert, Nevada, USA.

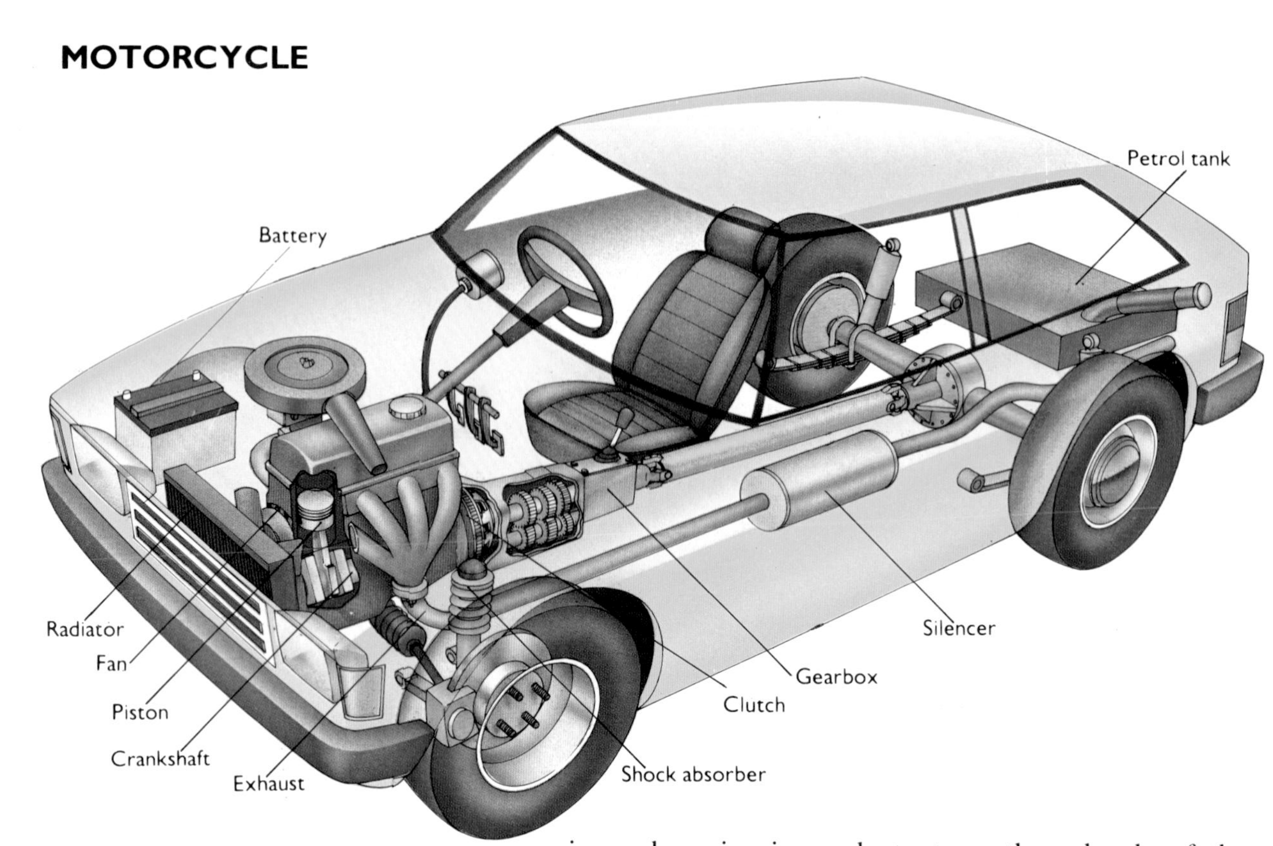

▲ *A cutaway of a modern motor car showing the main parts. Power produced by the engine is transmitted to the driving wheels. For most cars these are the rear wheels, although some cars use the front or all four as driving wheels.*

again and again, is made to turn the wheels of the car. (You can read more about this in the article on the INTERNAL COMBUSTION ENGINE.) The driver can make the car go faster by pressing the *accelerator* pedal. This makes more petrol go into the engine.

Cars are pushed along by either their front or back wheels. The engine is usually at the front. As the engine's *pistons* go up and down, they turn the *crankshaft*. The crankshaft is joined to the *clutch* and the *gearbox*, as you can see in the picture. The clutch cuts off the engine from the gearbox. When the driver presses the clutch pedal, the crankshaft is separated from the GEARS. Then the driver can safely change into another gear. If the driver wants maximum power he or she uses a low gear – first gear. The car needs plenty of power for starting or going up a steep hill. When the driver travels along a clear road at speed he or she uses top gear.

▼ *Early motorcycles, such as this Daimler of 1885, were very simple, slow and uncomfortable to ride.*

Motorcycle

The first motorcycle was built in 1885 by the German Gottlieb Daimler. He fitted one of his petrol engines to a wooden bicycle frame. Today's motorcycles are more complicated machines. The engine is similar to that of a car, but smaller. (See

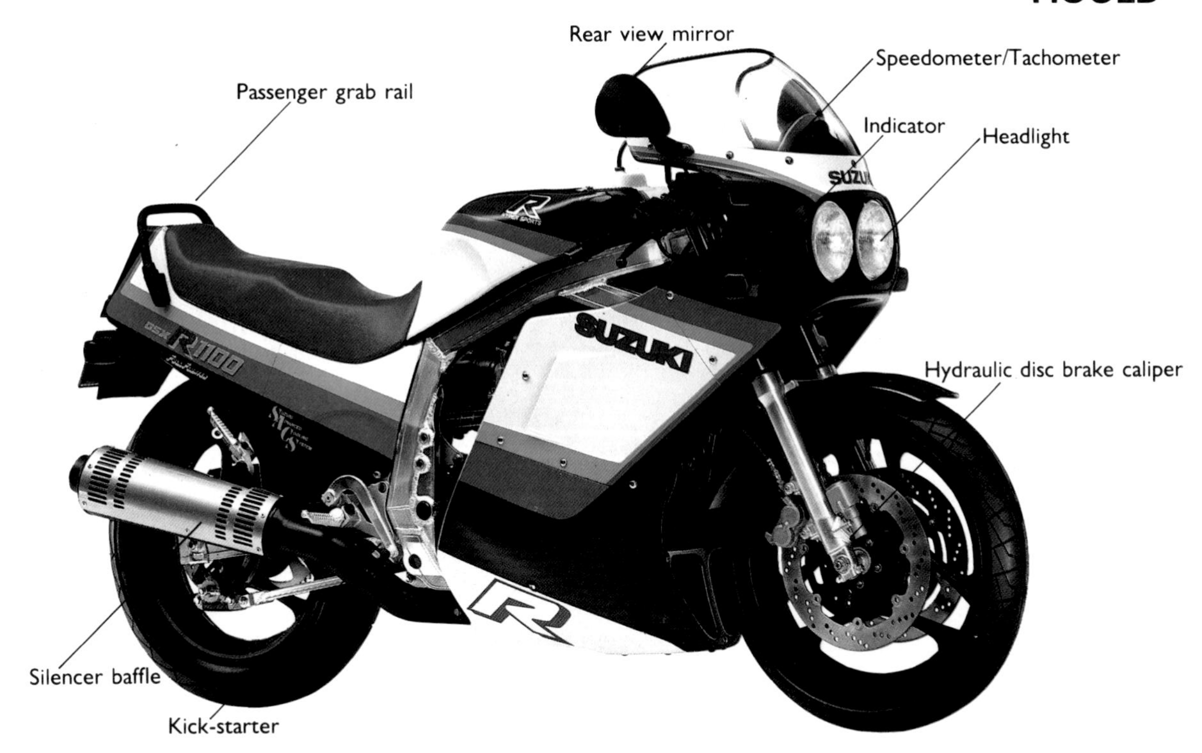

INTERNAL COMBUSTION ENGINE.) It is either a two-stroke or a four-stroke engine, and it may have from one to four cylinders. The engine can be cooled by either air or water. It is started with an ignition button on the handlebars. This turns the engine and starts it firing. The speed is controlled by a twist-grip on the handlebars. The clutch works from a hand lever. The gears are changed by a foot lever. Another foot pedal works the brake on the back wheel. A chain or drive shaft connects the engine to the back wheel and drives it round.

▲ *This Suzuki GSXR1100 has a maximum speed of 240 km/h and is designed for high-speed road use. Its engine is as big as that in many small family cars.*

Mould

Moulds are tiny plants that belong to the same group as the MUSHROOM. Unlike green plants, they cannot make their own food. They live on food made by other plants or animals. Moulds grow from a tiny particle called a *spore*. If a spore comes to rest on a piece of damp bread, it grows fine threads and starts to spread. Mouldy food should be thrown away. But some moulds are useful. Certain cheeses such as Stilton, Camembert and Roquefort get their flavour from the moulds that grow in them. The mould *Penicillium* is used for making the powerful germ-killing drug penicillin.

▼ *Some cheeses are treated with a* penicillium *mould to give them their special flavour and appearance.*

WORLD'S HIGHEST MOUNTAINS		
Peak	**Range**	**Metres**
Everest	Himalayas	8848
Godwin Austen	Karakoram	8610
Kanchen junga	Himalayas	8598
Lhotse	Himalayas	8510
Makalu	Himalayas	8470
Dhaulagiri I	Himalayas	8172
Manaslu	Himalayas	8156
Cho Oyu	Himalayas	8153
Nanga Parbat	Himalayas	8126
Annapurna I	Himalayas	8078
Gasherbrum I	Karakoram	8068
Broad Peak	Karakoram	8047
Gasherbrum II	Karakoram	8033
Gosainthan	Himalayas	8013
Gasherbrum III	Karakoram	7952
Annapurna II	Himalayas	7937
Gasherbrum IV	Karakoram	7925
Kangbachen	Himalayas	7902
Gyachung Kang	Himalayas	7897
Himal Chuli	Himalayas	7893
Disteghil Sar	Karakoram	7885
Kunyang Kish	Karakoram	7852
Dakum (Peak 29)	Himalayas	7852
Nuptse	Himalayas	7841

Mountain

A large part of the Earth's surface is covered by mountains. The greatest mountain ranges are the ALPS of Europe, the ROCKIES and the ANDES of America and the HIMALAYAS of Asia. The Himalayas are the greatest of them all. They have many of the world's highest peaks, including the biggest, Mount EVEREST.

There are mountains under the sea, too. And sometimes the peaks of under-sea mountains stick up above the sea's surface as islands. One mountain called Mauna Loa which rises from the floor of the Pacific Ocean is very much higher than Everest.

Mountains are formed by movements in the Earth's crust. Some mountains are formed when two great land masses move toward each other and squeeze up the land in between. The Alps were made in this way. Other mountains are VOLCANOES, great heaps of ash and lava that poured out when the volcano erupted.

But even the greatest mountains do not last for ever. The hardest rock gets worn away in time by rain, wind, sun and frost. RIVERS cut valleys, GLACIERS grind their way down, wearing away the mountains after untold centuries into gentle hills.

When the height of a mountain is given, it means the height above sea level. This can be a lot more than the height from the base.

▼ *Different plants grow at different altitudes in mountain areas. This is because the air gets thinner and colder the higher you go.*

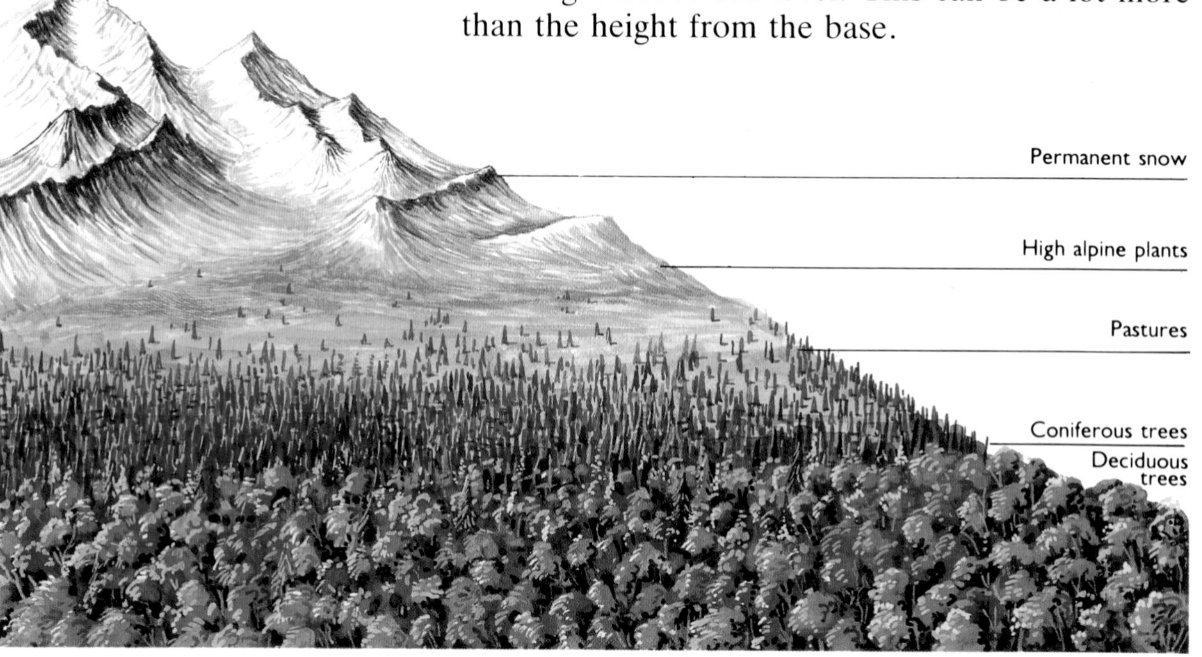

▲ *Mice are adaptable creatures and live in a variety of habitats.*

Mouse

A mouse is a RODENT, like its relative the RAT. And, like the rat, the house mouse is a pest to human beings. It can do a great deal of damage to stores of food, usually at night. One mouse can have 40 babies a year, and when the young are 12 weeks old they can themselves breed. People have used cats to catch mice for thousands of years. The wood mouse, field mouse, harvest mouse, and dormouse are mice that live in the countryside. White mice can be kept as pets.

Mozambique

Mozambique is a republic in East Africa. It was ruled by Portugal but became independent in 1975. Farming is the most important industry in this hot, tropical country. Mozambique's ports of Maputo and Beira are important for importing and exporting goods to the African interior.

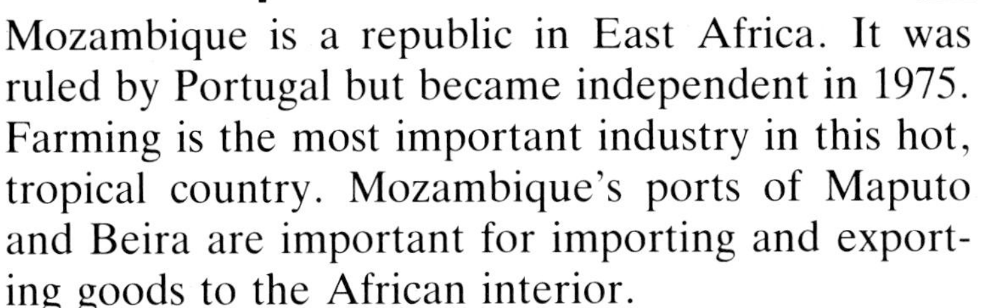

Most of the people of Mozambique are black Africans who speak one of several Bantu languages. There are also some Portuguese and Asians.

In the 1980s, severe droughts and civil war caused hardship in the country.

MOZAMBIQUE

ZAIRE
TANZANIA
COMOROS
ZAMBIA
MALAWI
ZIMBABWE
MOZAMBIQUE
MOZAMBIQUE CHANNEL
MADAGASCAR
BOTSWANA
INDIAN OCEAN
REPUBLIC OF SOUTH AFRICA
SWAZILAND

Government: Socialist one-party state
Capital: Maputo
Area: 783,030 sq km
Population: 15,656,000
Language: Portuguese
Currency: Metical

▲ *From a very early age, Mozart was taken on concert tours by his father Leopold, also a musician.*

Mozart, Wolfgang Amadeus

Wolfgang Amadeus Mozart (1756–1791) was an Austrian and one of the greatest composers of music that the world has known. He began writing music at the age of five. Two years later he was playing at concerts all over Europe. Mozart wrote over 600 pieces of music, including many beautiful operas and symphonies. But he earned little money from his hard work. He died in poverty at the age of 35.

Muhammad

Muhammad (AD 570–632) was the founder and leader of the RELIGION known as ISLAM. He was born in MECCA in what is now Saudi Arabia. At the age of 40 he believed that God had asked him to preach to the ARABS. He taught that there was only one God, called Allah.

In 622 he was forced out of Mecca, and this is the year from which the Muslim calendar dates. After his death his teachings spread rapidly across the world.

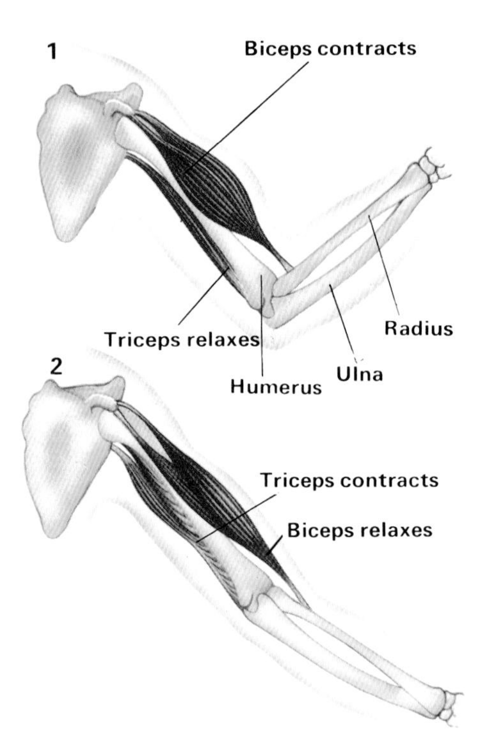

▲ *Muscles often work in pairs, with one contracting as the other relaxes. They are said to be* antagonistic, *or working against each other. This is how the arm muscles work.*

Muscle

Muscles are the things that make the parts of our bodies move. When you pick up this book or kick a ball you are using muscles. There are two different kinds of muscles. Some work when your brain tells them to. When you pick up a chair, your brain sends signals to muscles in your arms, in your body and in your legs. All these muscles work together at the right time, and you pick up the chair. Other kinds of muscles work even when you are asleep. Your stomach muscles go on churning the food you have eaten. Your heart muscles go on pumping blood. The human body has more than 500 muscles.

Mushroom and Toadstool

Mushrooms grow in woods, fields and on people's lawns – almost anywhere, in fact, where it is warm enough and damp enough. Some mushrooms are very good to eat. Others are so poisonous that people die from eating them. Many people call the poisonous ones toadstools. Mushrooms are in the FUNGUS group of plants. They have no green colouring matter (CHLOROPHYLL); instead they feed on decayed matter in the soil or on other plants.

▲ *Poisonous toadstools like these sometimes look dangerous, but even some harmless-looking ones can kill.*

Music

People have been making some kind of music all through history. The very earliest people probably made singing noises and beat time with pieces of wood. We know that the ancient Egyptians enjoyed their music. Paintings in the tombs of the PHARAOHS show musicians playing pipes, harps and other stringed instruments. The ancient Greeks also liked stringed instruments such as the lyre. But we have no idea what this early music sounded like, because there was no way of writing it down.

By the MIDDLE AGES, composers were writing music for groups of instruments. But it was not until the 1600s that the ORCHESTRA as we know it was born. The first orchestras were brought together by Italian composers to accompany their OPERAS. It was at this time that VIOLINS, violas and cellos were first used.

As instruments improved, new ones were added to the orchestra. BACH and HANDEL, who were both born in 1685, used orchestras with mostly stringed instruments like the violin. But they also had flutes, oboes, trumpets and horns. Joseph HAYDN was the first composer to use the orchestra as a whole. He invented the *symphony*. In this, all the instruments

▼ *In music some notes have two names. C sharp, for instance, is the same note as D flat. A ♯ by a note means that it is raised by a semi-tone, a ♭ by a note means it is lowered a semi-tone.*

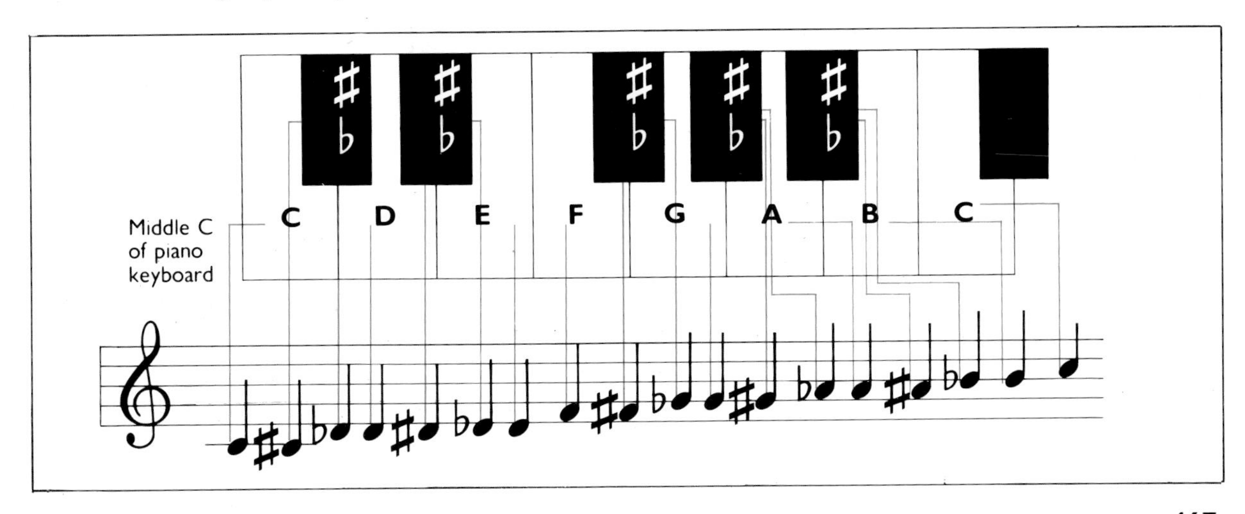

► *The layout of a modern symphony orchestra has been developed over many years.*

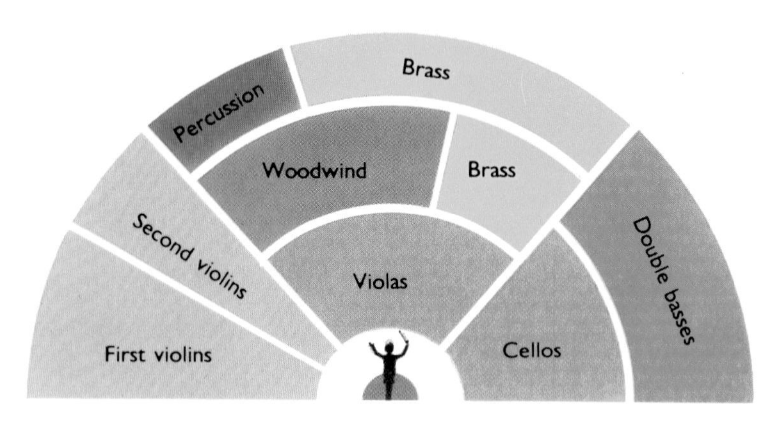

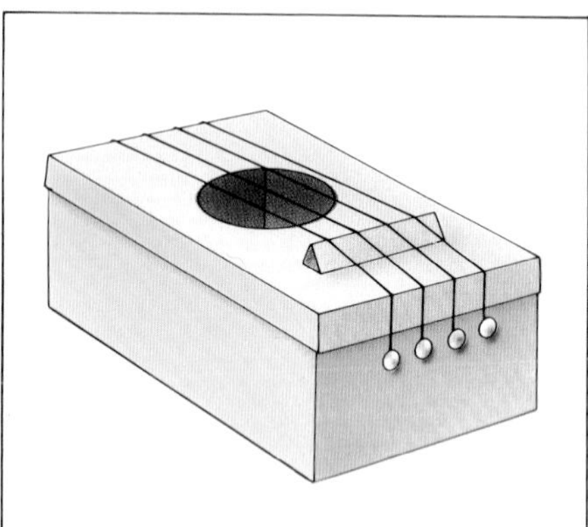

SEE IT YOURSELF

You can make a simple guitar from a cardboard box and some elastic bands. Cut a hole in the lid of the box and tack lengths of elastic of varying thickness tightly across it. Fit a wedge of wood beneath the elastic bands as shown. The bands will give out different notes when they are plucked.

blended together so that none was more important than the others.

A new kind of music began with the great German composer BEETHOVEN. He began writing music in which some of the notes clashed. This sounded rather shocking to people who listened to his music in his day. Later musicians tried all kinds of mixtures of instruments. In the 1900s new kinds of music were made by composers such as Igor Stravinsky and Arnold Schoenberg. Others since then have used tape recorders and electronic systems to produce new sounds which are often rather strange to our ears.

But much music still has three things: *melody, harmony* and *rhythm*. The melody is the tune. Harmony is the agreeable sound made when certain notes are played together. Often these notes form a *chord*, an arrangement of notes within a particular musical key. Rhythm is the regular 'beat' of the music. The simplest kind of music is just beating out a rhythm on a drum.

What is probably the oldest kind of musical instrument has been found by archaeologists in Stone Age sites. It is a bull-roarer, consisting of a small oval-shaped piece of bone with a hole in one end in which a cord is tied. It is whirled around by the player and produces a buzzing sound – the faster it is whirled, the higher the buzz.

Musical Instrument

There are four kinds of musical instrument. In wind instruments, air is made to vibrate inside a tube. This vibrating air makes a musical note.

All *woodwind* instruments such as clarinets, bassoons, flutes, piccolos and recorders have holes that are covered by the fingers or by pads worked by the fingers. These holes change the length of the vibrating column of air inside the instrument. The shorter the column the higher the note. In *brass* wind instruments, the vibration of the player's lips makes the air in the instrument vibrate. By changing the pressure of the lips, the player can make different notes. Most brass instruments also have valves and pistons to change the length of the vibrating column of air, and so make different notes.

Stringed instruments work in one of two ways. The strings of the instrument are either made to vibrate by a bow, as in the violin, viola, cello and double bass; or the strings are plucked, as in the guitar, harp or banjo.

In *percussion* instruments, a tight piece of skin or a piece of wood or metal is struck to make a note. There are lots of percussion instruments – drums, cymbals, gongs, tambourines, triangles and chimes.

Electronic instruments such as the electric organ and the synthesizer make music using sounds produced by electronic circuits.

▼ *Percussion instruments are played by striking them. The note made by the timpani can be changed by tightening or loosening the skin.*

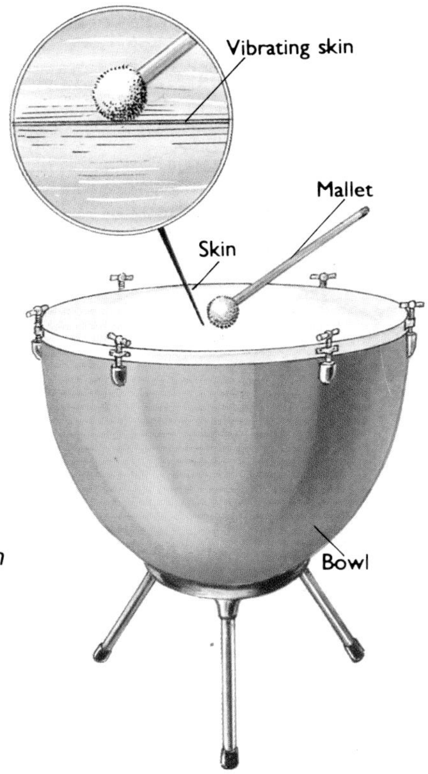

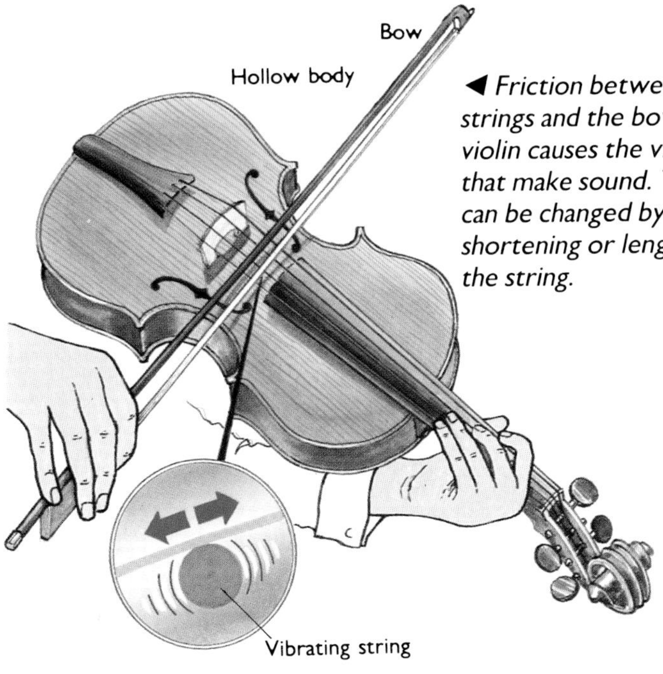

◀ *Friction between the strings and the bow of a violin causes the vibrations that make sound. The pitch can be changed by shortening or lengthening the string.*

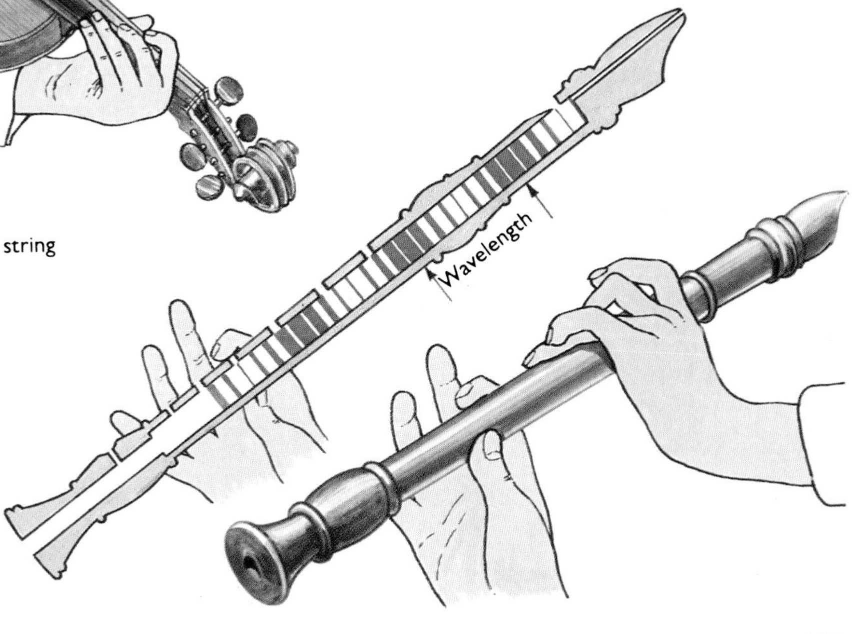

▶ *By covering the holes on a recorder, different notes are produced by the air in the column, which vibrates when blown.*

▲ *Mussolini was known in his native Italy as* Il Duce, *which means 'the leader'.*

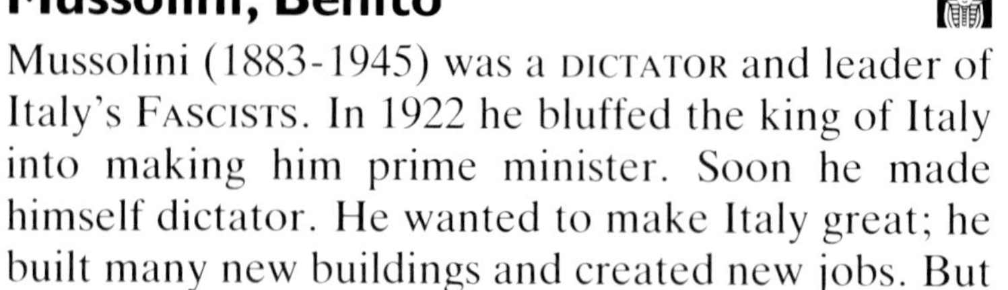

Mussolini, Benito

Mussolini (1883-1945) was a DICTATOR and leader of Italy's FASCISTS. In 1922 he bluffed the king of Italy into making him prime minister. Soon he made himself dictator. He wanted to make Italy great; he built many new buildings and created new jobs. But he also wanted military glory and led Italy into World War II on the side of HITLER. His armies were defeated by the Allies and Mussolini was finally captured and shot by his own people.

Myth

In ancient times, people believed that the world was inhabited by many different gods and spirits. There were gods of war and thunder, the sea, wine and hunting. The Sun and the Moon were gods too. Stories that tell of the gods are called myths. The study of myths is called mythology.

Some myths tell of extraordinary human beings called *heroes* who performed great deeds. Others tell of the tricks the gods played on ordinary mortals. There are myths from all countries, but those of Greece and Rome have become the most familiar. Many of the Greek myths were adopted by the Romans. They even adopted some of the Greek gods.

Mythology teaches us much about the way people of long ago thought and lived.

▼ *The ancient Egyptians believed in many gods. Some were represented with the heads of animals considered sacred by the Egyptians. Osiris, god of the afterlife, was married to Isis, goddess of female fertility, and Horus was their son. Anubis escorted the dead to the afterworld, and Re was the Sun god.*

Horus

Anubis

Isis

Osiris

Re

Nail and Claw

Nails and claws are made of hard skin, like animals' horns. They grow at the end of toes and fingers. When they are broad and flat they are called nails, but if they are sharp and pointed they are claws. Human nails are of little use. But BIRDS, MAMMALS and REPTILES use their claws to attack and to defend themselves.

A close look at an animal's claws will tell you about its way of life. CATS and birds of prey have very sharp claws. They are hooked for holding onto and tearing prey. ANTEATERS have long, strong, curved claws for tearing apart termites' nests.

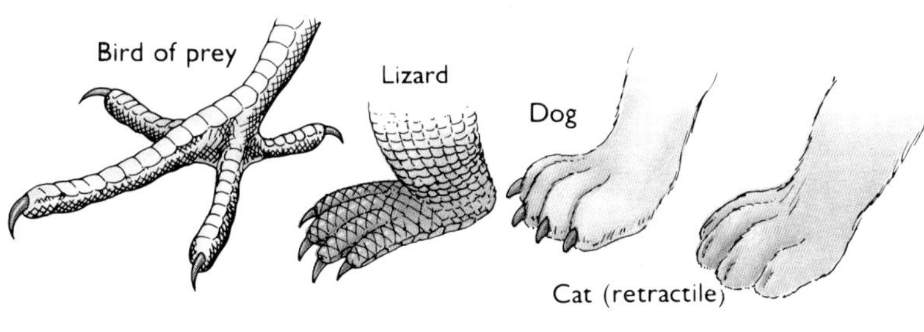

◄ The claws of birds, reptiles and mammals are all vital to their survival. The claw design of members of the cat family is particularly interesting. The claws can be retracted (pulled back) into the paws at will.

Namibia

Namibia is in the south-west part of Africa. On some maps the country is called South West Africa. Most of the country is a plateau more than 1000 metres high. In the east is a part of the Kalahari Desert. There is not much good farmland. The main industry is mining.

In 1915, the country became a South African territory under the League of Nations. In 1946, the United Nations said that South Africa had no rights over Namibia, but South Africa disputed this. In 1989 it was finally agreed that South Africa would hand over power to the black majority. Independence was achieved in 1990.

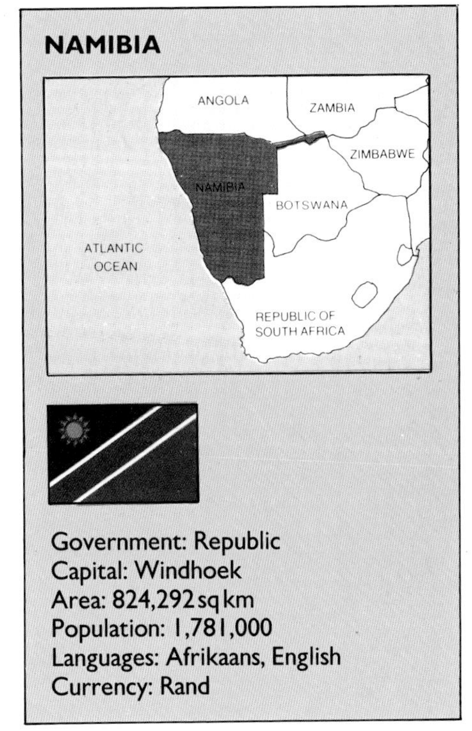

Napoleon Bonaparte

In 1789 the people of France rebelled against the unjust rule of their king and his nobles. The FRENCH REVOLUTION was supported by a young man born on the island of Corsica 20 years before. His name was Napoleon Bonaparte (1769–1821).

► *Napoleon set out to conquer the whole of Europe. Shown here is the extent of his empire at the height of his power.*

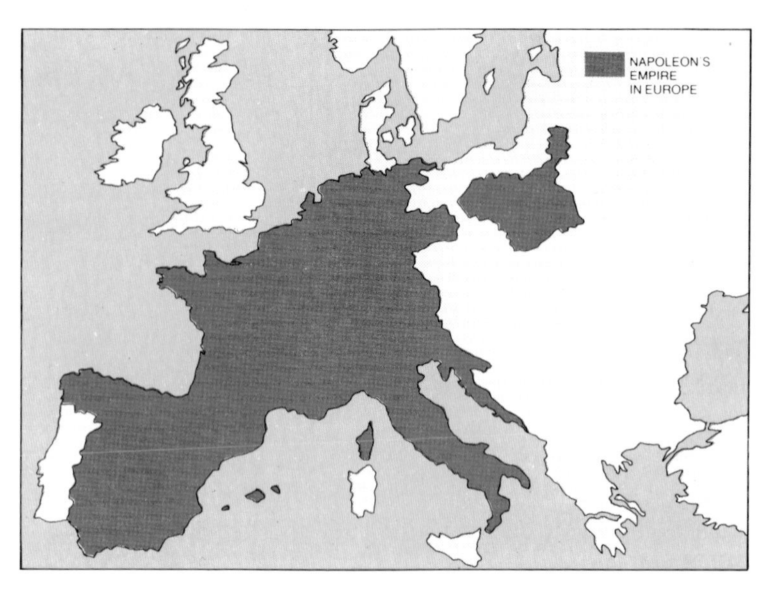

As the pope prepared to crown Napoleon emperor in Notre Dame cathedral, Napoleon seized the crown from his hands and placed it on his own head, to show that he, Napoleon, had personally gained the right to wear it.

Napoleon went to the leading military school in Paris, and by 1792 he was a captain of artillery. Three years later he saved France by crushing a royalist rebellion in Paris. Soon Napoleon was head of the French army and won great victories in Italy, Belgium and Austria. In 1804 he crowned himself emperor of France in the presence of the Pope. Then he crowned his wife, Josephine.

But Napoleon could not defeat Britain at sea. He tried to stop all countries from trading with Britain, but Russia would not cooperate. So Napoleon led a great army into Russia in the winter of 1812. This campaign ended in disaster. His troops were defeated by the bitter weather. Then he met his final defeat at the battle of WATERLOO in 1815. There he was beaten by the British under WELLINGTON and the Prussians under Blücher. He was made prisoner by the British on the lonely Atlantic island of St Helena, where he died in 1821.

Napoleon was a small man. His soldiers adored him and called him 'the little corporal'. Napoleon drew up a new French code of law. Many of his laws are still in force today.

▲ *With political skills equal to his skills as a general, Napoleon reorganized the government of France.*

NATO (North Atlantic Treaty Organization)

NATO is a defensive alliance set up after World War II. In 1949, 12 countries signed a treaty in which they agreed that an attack on one member should be considered an attack on them all. The 12 were Belgium, Canada, Denmark, France, Iceland, Italy, Luxembourg, the Netherlands, Norway, Portugal, the United Kingdom and the United States. Greece and Turkey joined in 1951, West Germany in 1954, and Spain in 1982. The original NATO headquarters were in Paris.

The purpose of the alliance is to unify and strengthen the military defences of the nations of Western Europe. Each member nation contributes soldiers and supplies to NATO forces. But the members of NATO also cooperate on political and economic issues.

In the 1960s some NATO members felt that the United States had too much power in the alliance. France withdrew her NATO forces in 1966. France is still a NATO member, but the headquarters have been moved from Paris to Brussels. With the collapse of many of the Communist governments of Eastern Europe in 1990, NATO is looking closely at its role for the future. In 1991 NATO forces were restructured as the Cold War came to an end. United States forces in Europe are being cut back.

In 1966, Charles de Gaulle announced France's withdrawal from NATO, though not from the Atlantic Alliance.

Natural Gas

Natural gas is a type of GAS which occurs naturally underground and does not have to be manufactured. It is usually found in OIL fields, but is sometimes found on its own. When there is only a little natural gas in an oil field, it is burned off. If there is plenty, it is piped away and used for cooking, heating and producing ELECTRICITY.

It is found in large quantities in Russia, in Texas and Louisiana in the United States, and in the NORTH SEA oil fields. Half the world's supply of natural gas is used by the United States.

Nauru

Nauru is a tiny island country in the Pacific Ocean. The only industry is mining for phosphate, but by the mid 1990s there will be no phosphate left on the island. Nauru became independent in 1968 and is a member of the Commonwealth.

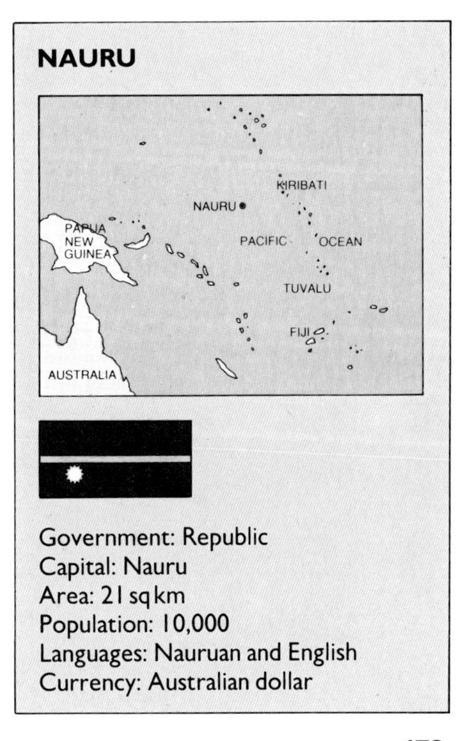

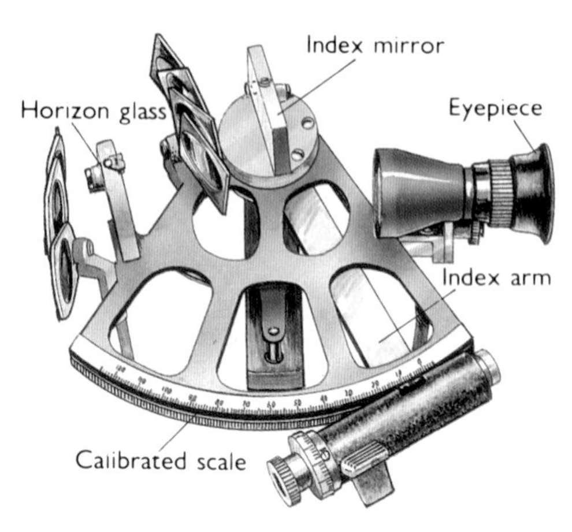

▲ *A sextant can be used to work out a ship's position by measuring the angle between a star or the Sun and the horizon (see below).*

Navigation

Navigation means finding the way, usually in a ship or an aircraft. For hundreds of years, navigators at sea used the changing positions of the Sun and stars to work out their LATITUDE. Knowing the difference between the time on the ship and the time set at 0° longitude at Greenwich helped them to work out their position more precisely.

Today, many navigational instruments are electronic and are very accurate. Radio beacons and SATELLITES send out signals from which a ship can find its position. Then the navigator uses a COMPASS to keep the ship on the right course. COMPUTERS help ships, aircraft and spacecraft navigate so exactly that their position is known precisely.

► *Once the angle has been measured, the star's position at that particular time can be looked up in a very accurate table. This allows the position of the ship to be calculated. By taking a series of sextant readings the ship can be kept on the right course.*

Nelson, Horatio

Horatio Nelson (1758–1805) was a famous British admiral at the time when Britain was at war with the French, led by NAPOLEON BONAPARTE.

Nelson was born in Norfolk, the son of a country clergyman. He joined the navy when he was 12 and was captain of a frigate by the time he was 20. He was made a rear-admiral in 1797. By then he had already lost an eye in battle. Soon he lost an arm too.

In 1798 he led his ships to victory against the French at Alexandria in Egypt. While he was in the Mediterranean he met and fell in love with Lady Hamilton, the wife of the British ambassador to Naples. Nelson loved Lady Hamilton all his life.

▲ *Nelson once ignored an order to stop an attack by pretending he couldn't see the signal – he held his telescope to his blind eye.*

Many people thought this was shocking as they were both married to other people.

Nelson's most famous battle was his last. It was fought against a French fleet led by Admiral Villeneuve. For nearly 10 months in 1805, Nelson's ships chased Villeneuve's across the Atlantic and back. Then, on October 21, they met off the Cape of Trafalgar in southern Spain. Nelson defeated the French in the battle that followed but was killed on board his ship, the *Victory*.

Before the battle Nelson sent a famous message to all the ships in his fleet: 'England expects that every man will do his duty.'

Nepal

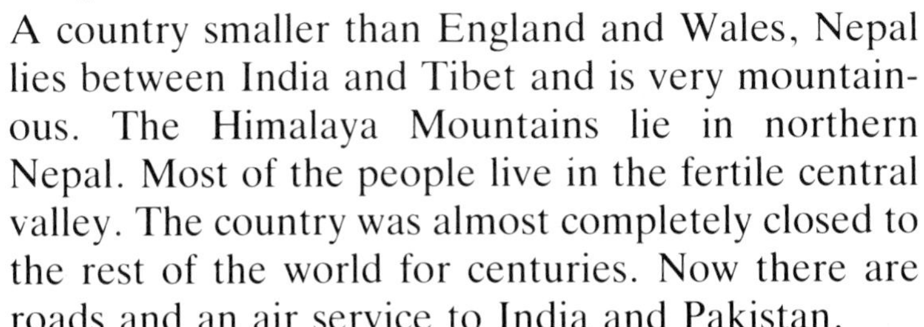

A country smaller than England and Wales, Nepal lies between India and Tibet and is very mountainous. The Himalaya Mountains lie in northern Nepal. Most of the people live in the fertile central valley. The country was almost completely closed to the rest of the world for centuries. Now there are roads and an air service to India and Pakistan.

NEPAL

Government: Constitutional monarchy
Capital: Katmandu
Area: 140,797 sq km
Population: 18,916,000
Language: Nepali
Currency: Rupee

Neptune (Planet)

The PLANET Neptune is named after the Roman god of water and the sea. It is a large planet far out in the SOLAR SYSTEM. It is about 4493 million km from the SUN. Only PLUTO is farther away. It takes Neptune 165 years to circle the Sun. (The Earth takes 365 days.)

▼ *If we could observe Neptune from its large moon, Triton, it would probably look like this. The light from the Sun would be no brighter than that of a star.*

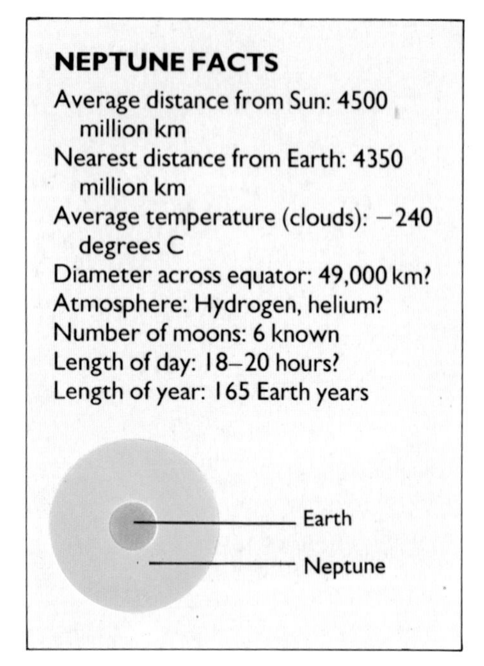

NEPTUNE FACTS

Average distance from Sun: 4500 million km
Nearest distance from Earth: 4350 million km
Average temperature (clouds): −240 degrees C
Diameter across equator: 49,000 km?
Atmosphere: Hydrogen, helium?
Number of moons: 6 known
Length of day: 18–20 hours?
Length of year: 165 Earth years

Being so far from the Sun, Neptune is a very cold place. Scientists think its atmosphere is rather like JUPITER's, which is mostly made up of the gas HYDROGEN. Neptune has six moons, and scientists have recently discovered a system of thin rings around the planet.

Early astronomers were unable to see Neptune, but they knew it had to be there. They could tell there was something affecting the ORBIT of the nearby planet URANUS. In 1845 two astronomers, Adams in England and Leverrier in France, used mathematics to work out where Neptune should be. Astronomers used this information the next year, and spotted Neptune.

Nerve

Nerves are tiny fibres made up of CELLS. They reach all through the body. When a part of the body touches something, the nerves send a message through the spinal column to the BRAIN. If we feel PAIN, a message is sent back to make us move away from whatever is hurting. Nerves also carry the senses of sight, hearing and taste. The sense organs have special nerve endings that respond to heat, light, cold and other stimuli around us.

▼ *If the size of the various parts of your body corresponded to the number of nerve cells in them, you would look rather like this.*

▼ *A motor nerve, with its many dendrites and long axon, carries messages from the brain or spinal cord to the muscles.*

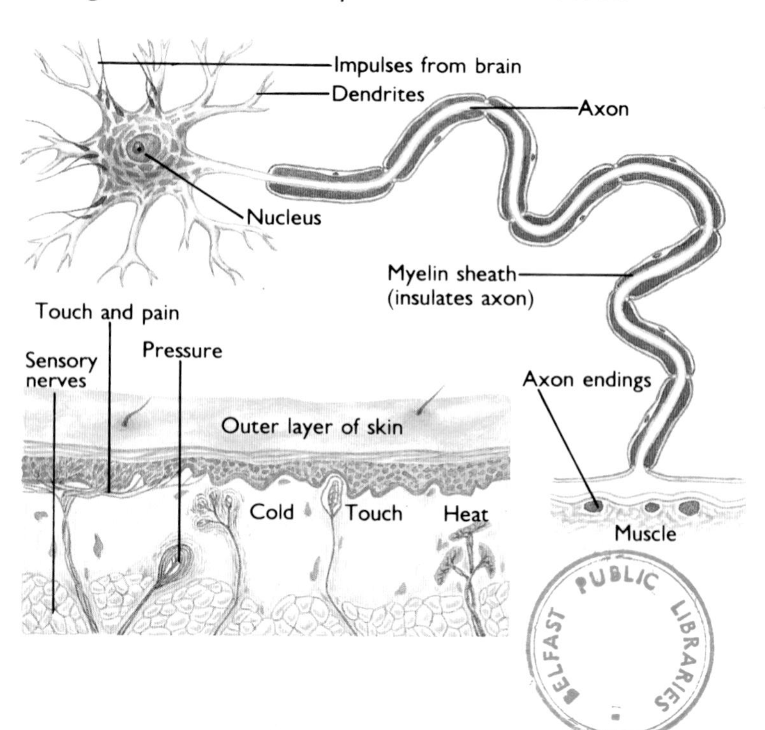

► *Various receptors in the skin deal with different sensations. They transmit these sensations to the brain with the help of nerve cells.*